THE APOLOGETICS OF THE EVANGELICAL RENAISSANCE

THE APOLOGETICS OF THE EVANGELICAL RENAISSANCE

THE QUEST FOR A GENERAL THEORY OF CHRISTIAN DEFENSE

Revised Edition

Max H. Sotak, Ph.D.

Sotakoff
Publishing

THE APOLOGETICS OF THE EVANGELICAL RENAISSANCE
The Quest for a General Theory of Christian Defense
Revised Edition
Max H. Sotak

ISBN-10: 0-9896808-7-8
ISBN-13: 978-0-9896808-7-5

© 2017 Max H. Sotak. All rights reserved worldwide.

Published by: Sotakoff Publishing

No part of this publication may be reproduced, stored in a retrieval system, or transmitted in any form or by any means—for example, electronics, photocopy, recording—without the prior written permission of the publisher. The only exception is brief quotations in printed reviews.

Scripture taken from the HOLY BIBLE, NEW INTERNATIONAL VERSION.
Copyright © 1973, 1978, 1984 International Bible Society.
Used by permission.

Contents

PREFACE VII
    PREFACE TO THE REVISED EDITION VIII

CHAPTER 1 11

A GENERAL SYNTHESIS OF APOLOGETICS 11

THE GUIDING PURPOSE 15
    The Goal of the Investigation 16
    The Central Questions of the Investigation 18

THE GUIDING ASSUMPTION 21
    The Unification of Apologetics 21
    Three Basic Presuppositional Categories 23

CHAPTER 2 27

A GENERAL SAMPLING OF APOLOGETICS I 27

TWO CATEGORICAL PRESUPPOSITIONALISTS 33
    J. Oliver Buswell 33
    Norman Geisler 40

CHAPTER 3 51

A GENERAL SAMPLING OF APOLOGETICS II 51

TWO ANALYTICAL PRESUPPOSITIONALISTS 51
    Edward Carnell 51
    Bernard Ramm 57

CHAPTER 4 67

A GENERAL SAMPLING OF APOLOGETICS III 67

TWO METAPHYSICAL PRESUPPOSITIONALISTS 67
    Cornelius Van Til 67
    John Frame 76

Chapter 5 87
A GENERAL METHOD FOR APOLOGETICS 87
A Balanced Approach to Pre-Cognitive Issues 88
A Theory of Philosophical Disagreements 89
Resolving Philosophical Disagreements 95
A Balanced Approach to Cognitive Issues 100
A Theory of Epistemic Disagreements 101
Resolving Epistemic Disagreements 103
Chapter 6 113
A GENERAL SUMMARY OF APOLOGETICS 113
The Synopsis of Apologetics 114
The Analysis of Apologetics 128
Method and Content.. 129
Categories and Hypotheses 131
Proof and Certainty 136
Experiential Presuppositionalism 139
Chapter 7.. 143
A GENERAL THEORY OF APOLOGETICS 143
A General Theory in Principle 144
A General Theory in Practice.. 150
Appendix... 157
THOM NOTARO'S *VAN TIL & THE USE OF EVIDENCE* 157
WORKS CITED... 161

Preface

I became a Christian in the wake of what has been called the Evangelical Renaissance of the early 1970's. What I did not know when I became a Christian during my senior year of high school was that evangelical Christians had been making intellectual investments in their movement and its institutions for several decades, attempting to distinguish themselves from theological liberals on the left and fundamentalists on the right. Through their educational institutions, publishers, and evangelistic efforts, evangelicals were succeeding in their defense and proclamation of the gospel to such an extent that George Gallup, Jr. named 1976 the "Year of the Evangelical." In God's providence, this gospel also came to me, a young person who had been secularized by the music and mentality of the 1960's and a philosophical father who had reacted against his own faith and upbringing as the son of a Russian Orthodox priest. A Harvard Divinity School education left my father a religious naturalist and the most ardent evolutionist I have ever known, and he preached his own version of sociobiology to his children with the evangelistic zeal of Billy Graham. The message was often elaborated in lengthy "sermons" after dinner: Adapt to the impersonal "design" of nature or die. Ironically, the graceless message of my father's naturalism made the gospel of grace stand out as unique, attractive, and true. Once I became convinced that the Bible is the Word of God, I believed.

Given my secular upbringing and a philosophical gene inherited from my father, I knew I would have to study my reasons for becoming a Christian as diligently as I began studying the Bible and my newfound theology. Evangelical publishers gave me access to the best in theology, apologetics, and biblical studies that had ever been available, and so I set out on a path of Christian scholarship that has been followed now for over forty years. An undergraduate degree in philosophy prepared me for graduate study in philosophy, apologetics, and theology, and the problems of philosophical apologetics became the task of a lifetime.

The following study attempts to accomplish what most apologists think is too audacious: To derive a general theory of Christian defense from the best systems offered by evangelical apologists during the fifty years from 1945 to 1995. The Evangelical Renaissance falls in the middle of this period and reflects the spiritual high point of evangelicalism in apologetic evangelism. In my judgment, this entire period represents the highest level of apologetic reflection in the history of Christianity thus far. This judgment is not based on the belief that any one apologist captured the truth, the whole truth, and nothing but the truth in apologetics; rather, the thinkers of this period engage in apologetic dialogue at a level of sophistication that makes the goal of a general theory of Christian defense possible. While a number of studies summarize and categorize the tremendous contributions of the period, there remains a need for a synthesis that does justice to the genius of argumentative apologetics in America during the second half of the 20th Century. It is my hope that this study will serve as a memorial to the great evangelical apologists who readily gave a reason for the hope that was in them and remains in us. If I am audacious in my goal, it is because of my confidence that these apologists provide for more than even they thought possible.

PREFACE TO THE REVISED EDITION

The revised edition of this book provides a clearer presentation of some of the more challenging issues within the book, especially those in the fifth chapter on epistemology. The original edition had as a goal to feature a more direct exposure to some of my sources to enable the reader to observe my dialogue and interaction with these sources more closely. Over time, however, it became evident to me that the clarity of the material in some sections of the book was not served by this strategy. Therefore, I have recast these sections with an eye to bringing out the content of my sources more clearly, rather than requiring my readers to switch frequently between my style and the many often difficult writing styles reflected in my sources. Overall, this has improved the flow of the argument and relieved difficulty at many points. A second reason for the revision was a sense that I had not done justice to the presuppositional position of John Frame. Clarifications of Frame, especially with respect to his very insightful treatment of the relationship between Christian evidence and arguments, was not consistent in the first edition with my subsequent treatment of him in my book, *Framing Francis Schaeffer: Apologetics and Personal Integrity*. I am glad to have had the opportunity to make these adjustments and to offer a more accurate and attainable account of the apologetics of the Evangelical Renaissance.

THE APOLOGETICS OF THE
EVANGELICAL RENAISSANCE

CHAPTER 1

A GENERAL SYNTHESIS OF APOLOGETICS

The use of presuppositions is one of the most hotly debated topics in apologetics. Indeed, the classification of apologetic systems is determined by what each method presupposes. Presuppositions also determine the standard of certainty in apologetics. The type of assumptions an apologist makes will entail a corresponding notion of certainty, ranging from practical probability to logical certainty. While some notable attempts have been made to unify Christian apologetics through a combinational approach, it is doubtful that a synthesis has been proposed that would satisfy most evangelical apologists.

According to John Warwick Montgomery, the rebirth of apologetics within Evangelicalism began in 1945 with the publication of Wilbur Smith's book, *Therefore Stand*.[1] Since then, a flood of books on apologetics has come forth representing some of the best Christian scholarship of the last century. While most notable apologists of the last century have built largely on historical methods, there has also been considerable creative reflection on the presuppositional foundations of apologetics. This reflection was no doubt stimulated by the "presuppositional" apologetic of Cornelius Van Til. Largely inspired by the idealistic philosophical climate of the early part of the 20th Century, Van Til's apologetic provoked a presuppositional awareness even among apologists who strongly disagreed with him. Achieving a clarified presuppositional self-consciousness among evangelical apologists is, in my opinion, one of the most important goals of apologetics.

The following study is an analysis of the use of presuppositions in apologetics for the purpose of synthesizing the major contributions into a general theory of apologetics. This is a feasible study for three reasons: (1) Excellent work has already been done analyzing the distinctions among apologists in their use of presuppositions, which has resulted in recog-

---

[1] John W. Montgomery, *A History of Apologetics Through the Centuries* (Class Syllabus: Trinity Theological Seminary, n.d.), 48.

nized presuppositional categories or schools of thought; (2) There are a number of prominent apologists who have developed typical expressions of each of these categories; (3) The more creative representatives of each school evidence a tendency to borrow from the other schools within the parameters of their own perspectives.

This third reason is especially important because it suggests the possibility of a theoretical synthesis. Based on an examination of the literature pertaining to this study, it is reasonable to believe that a synthesis is possible. While the representatives on the extreme ends of the presuppositional spectrum might not agree, the evidence suggests that it is possible to develop a consistent presuppositional theory that accounts for the different ways presuppositions operate in apologetics. If different apologetic methods have something to contribute to the overall task of apologetics, then a general theory of apologetics must be rich enough to comprehend most of those contributions. Given the philosophical context in which contemporary evangelical approaches have developed, a presuppositional viewpoint is perhaps the most fitting and appropriate vantage point from which to attack the problem of a synthesis.

An apologetic synthesis could also be conceived along more practical lines in which evidences and arguments are viewed in light of their apologetic results.[2] This person-centered approach focuses on the issues of communication and persuasion, not theoretical underpinnings. While this proposal is useful, it appeals to a practical view of unity, whereas a presuppositional analysis appeals to a theoretical view of unity.

The value of an apologetic synthesis is based on its relevance to the areas of evangelism and Christian unity. It goes without saying that evangelism today requires apologetics. Postmodern pluralism has fragmented the non-Christian mind into a variety of belief systems that Christians must be able to confront effectively with the gospel. Therefore, a person-centered approach to apologetics is clearly relevant today. In fact, the biblical witness demonstrates that the gospel is to be defended according to the background of the audience, not the philosophical preferences of the evangelist. If we are to become all things to all men, we must have a theory of apologetics that makes it possible to appeal to those of all philosophical temperaments and mindsets. While it is possible to be pragmatic about

---

[2] Cf. Alister E. McGrath, *Intellectuals Don't Need God & Other Modern Myths: Building Bridges to Faith Through Apologetics* (Grand Rapids: Zondervan Publishing House, 1993), 11.

apologetics and recommend whatever works in the situation, it is also helpful to attempt to uncover the theoretical underpinnings of what works in practice. Perhaps there is an underlying unity to major approaches that not only validates them but also provides a basis for extending them beyond their limited boundaries. The premise of this study is that presuppositions are at the heart of this quest for theoretical unity.

This study also has ecumenical value in that its purpose is not to propose another exclusive paradigm from which to criticize all others. Rather, its purpose is to build on the gains of the past by providing a theory that allows for the proper integration of those gains without contradictions, unnecessary limits, or inadequate concepts. Being human, apologists fall victim to their own philosophical predispositions and influences. Some are empirically minded while others think like idealists. Hence, apologetic systems are often little more than private epistemologies. The problem is not that apologists have differing frames of mind; difficulties arise when they cannot get outside their own perspectives to appreciate other frames of mind that may actually be compatible with their own. Because apologetics must address all mentalities, the individual apologist must be a person of the broadest sympathies. In short, whatever his personal preferences, the apologist must be a combinationalist at heart, or he will likely overlook many useful apologetic tools. Through a presuppositional theory, apologists may be brought together under a common cause that allows for both individuality and comprehensiveness.

General apologetic theories based on presuppositions are not common in the apologetic literature. With the exception of the presuppositional school of Van Til, only a few apologists have chosen to make presuppositions the heart of a general theory of apologetics. Edward Carnell stressed the role of presuppositions due to the influence of Van Til, under whom he studied.[3] Francis Schaeffer was also a student of Van Til.[4-5] While presuppositions were a major concern for both Carnell and Schaeffer, Van Til saw little resembling his own approach in either of his students. Gordon Clark

---

[3] Edward J. Carnell, An *Introduction to Christian Apologetics* (Grand Rapids: Wm. B. Eerdmans Publishing Company, 1948).

[4] Francis A. Schaeffer, *The Francis A. Schaeffer Trilogy* (Wheaton: Crossway Books, 1990).

[5] E. John Voss, *The Apologetics of Francis Schaeffer* (Th.D. diss., Dallas Theological Seminary, 1984).

and Carl Henry developed a rational presuppositionalism, which begins with the Trinity and ends with the law of contradiction.[6-7] Unlike Van Til, they were willing to test the Christian presupposition and all other presuppositions by a rational principle. Van Til's theory of apologetics was critical and exclusive.[8] Differing views of presuppositions held by his students or opponents were denounced as unscriptural concessions to autonomy. He made no attempt to synthesize the insights of traditional apologists with his own, believing them to be fatally flawed at the outset.

Outside the presuppositional school, one notable apologist has attempted to schematize apologetic methodology according to presuppositions. Stuart Hackett classified apologetic systems according to a threefold division based on how presuppositions are used and held.[9-10] The specifics of Hackett's classification will be discussed below. Charles Horne has also used this classification, for which he gives credit to Hackett.[11] Horne's use of Hackett's scheme serves a critical purpose to establish the superiority of Van Til's presuppositionalism over the approach of Carnell and others outside the presuppositional camp. Like Van Til and Horne, Hackett was also not concerned to use his analysis for the purpose of proposing a presuppositional synthesis. Like most of his evangelical contemporaries, he was also polarized on the question of presuppositions.

---

[6] Gordon H. Clark, *Religion, Reason and Revelation* (Jefferson, MD: The Trinity Foundation, 1986).

[7] Carl F. H. Henry, *Remaking the Modern Mind* (Grand Rapids: Wm. B. Eerdmans Publishing Co., 1946).

[8] Cornelius Van Til, *The Defense of the Faith* (Philadelphia: Presbyterian and Reformed Publishing Company, 1955). All page references correspond to the original unabridged 1955 edition.

[9] Stuart C. Hackett, *The Resurrection of Theism* (Chicago: Moody Press, 1957), 154ff.

[10] Stuart C. Hackett, *The Reconstruction of the Christian Revelation Claim: A Philosophical and Critical Apologetic* (Grand Rapids: Baker Book House, 1984).

[11] Charles M. Horne, "Van Til and Carnell—Part II," in *Jerusalem and Athens: Critical Discussions on the Theology and Apologetics of Cornelius Van Til*, ed. E. R. Geehan (Philadelphia: Presbyterian and Reformed Publishing Company, 1971), 379.

THE GUIDING PURPOSE

The purpose of this study is to develop a general theory of apologetics based on presuppositions. Such a theory would provide a critical theory by which other systems may be evaluated. If all the necessary concepts and distinctions are developed correctly, this study will serve as a useful analytical tool for problem solving in apologetics. The effectiveness of the theory may be tested by two criteria: (1) Explanatory Value—Does the theory explain the similarities and differences among the apologetic options? (2) Heuristic Value—Does the theory suggest new insights and possibilities through its application to the apologetic options? It is important to distinguish at this point between a general theory of apologetics and the many evidences commonly used by the apologist. Evidences are the raw materials of apologetics; a general theory is the blueprint for integrating these evidences and determining exactly what they justify.

What does it mean to justify belief? Apologists speak of justified belief in terms of proof or warrant. Proof is the evidence required to justify and compel belief. Proof may be viewed from two perspectives. On the one hand, proof is subjective and person-relative. The evidence required to justify a belief like the resurrection of Christ differs from person to person on the basis of many factors. On the other hand, proof is also objective in the sense that arguments may be offered for what should be considered adequate evidence for a specific belief. In fact, all apologists deal with proof from the objective perspective because they are not merely concerned with what evidence justifies a belief for them; they are also concerned with whether or not that evidence should compel belief in others.

Speaking of belief as *warranted* by the evidence represents an attempt to separate out the person-relativity of proof in favor of the objective merits of the evidence. Advocates of warrant strive for an argument that may be rejected but not refuted, believing that spiritual and moral factors ultimately determine whether or not one believes. A warranted belief, however, also involves a person (the apologist) who judges that a belief is warranted by the evidence. Thus, warrant is also person-relative, but to a lesser degree. The hostile non-Christian might reject the warrant for a belief for the same reason he would reject the proof for it: The evidence does not warrant belief for him.

Warrant has a more modest connotation than proof, but neither concept avoids person-relativity. The word *proof* connotes the idea that the evidence warrants belief and compels reasonable people to accept it. The rejection of proof does not necessarily indicate a failure in making a case;

rather, it indicates a failure in responding to the case by embracing a warranted belief. Thus, proof has an explicit deontological element that is either implicit in warrant or lacking altogether. Generally speaking, the apologist who believes that faith requires more than arguments and evidences will opt for warrant; the apologist who believes that faith arises on the basis of arguments and evidences will opt for proof.

The Goal of the Investigation

Recent scholarship in apologetics is provocative and diverse. Most apologists appreciate for the need for a comprehensive apologetic that is audience-oriented.[12] The continued relevance of Francis Schaeffer and C.S. Lewis is evidence that flexibility and a wide range of resources are understood to be absolutely necessary.[13] These trends, however, probably reflect more sensitivity to the practical demands of the apologetic task. The theoretical problem of supporting diverse methods and practices is another matter altogether.

Two apologists in particular seem especially concerned to develop a solid theoretical foundation for a comprehensive apologetic. Ronald Mayers has attempted to bridge the gap between Evidentialism and Presuppositionalism in his book, *Both/And: A Balanced Apologetic*.[14] This is a very helpful book, but it is meant to be a good general introduction to the practice of apologetics. Methodological questions do not receive enough attention to point the way to a full synthesis. Another popular book that is more suggestive of answers to the methodological problems is John Frame's *Apologetics to the Glory of God*.[15] Unlike Van Til, his mentor, Frame is more concerned to validate as much of traditional apologetics as possible within the constraints of his own position. While he does

---

[12] Cf. David K. Clark, *Dialogical Apologetics: A Person-Centered Approach to Christian Defense* (Grand Rapids: Baker Book House, 1993).

[13] Scott R. Burson, Jerry L. Walls, *C.S. Lewis & Francis Schaeffer: Lessons for a New Century from the Most Influential Apologists of Our Time* (Downers Grove: InterVarsity Press, 1998).

[14] Ronald B. Mayers, *Both/And: A Balanced Apologetic* (Chicago: Moody Press, 1984).

[15] John M. Frame, *Apologetics to the Glory of God: An Introduction* (Phillipsburg: Presbyterian and Reformed Publishing Company, 1994).

A General Synthesis of Apologetics 17

not propose a synthesis in this book or his two larger works on apologetics, the ecumenical motivation is evident in all he writes.[16-17]

Winfried Corduan makes an interesting contribution to the idea of a comprehensive apologetic by incorporating transcendental logic in his own version of the cosmological argument.[18] The desire to add the presuppositional emphasis on transcendental argument to a traditional approach is likely based, in Corduan's case, on the fact that he is a former presuppositionalist.[19] His version of Thomas' argument suggests that there is a connection between traditional cosmological reasoning and transcendental argumentation. Francis Schaeffer also explored the possibilities of this connection in his book, *He is There and He is Not Silent*. In a critical comment on this book, Robert Reymond referred to Schaeffer's argument as "the old cosmological argument of Thomas in new garb."[20] According to Corduan and Schaeffer, cosmological reasoning based on first principles is compatible with transcendental logic.

The goal of this study is to go beyond other apologists in specifying what makes a combinational system possible: *The very notion of presuppositional argumentation requires commitment to epistemological first principles and vice-versa.* Most Christian apologists reduce the controversy over presuppositions of method and content to an either/or issue. A contribution to apologetic method has yet to be made in the *explicit* argument that method and content are mutually dependent, and yet they may also witness to the truth on their own.[21] Some of the better apologists

---

[16] John M. Frame, *Cornelius Van Til: An Analysis of His Thought* (Phillipsburg: Presbyterian and Reformed Publishing Company, 1995).

[17] John M. Frame, *The Doctrine of the Knowledge of God* (Phillipsburg: Presbyterian and Reformed Publishing Company, 1987).

[18] Winfried Corduan, *Reasonable Faith: Basic Christian Apologetics* (Nashville: Broadman & Holman Publishers, 1993), 108-121.

[19] Winfried Corduan, review of *Apologetics To the Glory of God*, by John Frame, in *Trinity Journal* 16NS (1995): 131.

[20] Robert L. Reymond, *The Justification of Knowledge* (Phillipsburg: Presbyterian and Reformed Publishing Co., 1976), 145.

[21] The idea that method and content can witness to the truth on their own may seem to imply the neutrality of epistemological first principles and truth tests, in which case it would be inconsistent to speak of the mutual dependence of method and content. While first principles and

recognize this to some degree, but the point should become an explicit guide for an apologetic method.

The affirmation that method and content are interrelated should not be taken as a reaffirmation of Van Til's view. It is not necessary to affirm, as Van Til does, that presupposing a specific content is the necessary starting point of apologetics. Nor does the thesis require the acceptance of all presuppositions of content as categorical and equally certain. What is required as a platform for this study is that a complete apologetic method must do justice to *both* presuppositions of method and content.

The Central Questions of the Investigation

Investigations are guided by questions, and the main question of this study is a methodological one designed to promote discovery: How might Stuart Hackett's presuppositional analysis be used to describe contemporary evangelical apologetics and to synthesize a general theory of apologetics? In answering this question, other subsidiary questions will be answered in the process: (1) How do apologetic systems differ in presuppositional scope, function, content and modality? (2) How do apologetic systems differ on the issue of common ground? (3) How do apologetic systems differ on the method of proof? (4) How do apologetic systems differ on the extent of proof? (5) What apologetical schools best exemplify Hackett's basic categories? (6) What major apologists best exemplify Hackett's basic categories? (7) What philosophical schools best exemplify Hackett's basic categories? (8) What major philosophers best exemplify Hackett's basic categories? (9) What conceptual adjustments are required

---

truth tests are not neutral, good and sufficient reasons can be given for their use prior to knowing what content must be presupposed in order to give an account of them. Predictive success and the practical reliability of knowing faculties instills a general confidence in most that knowledge is possible, and Scripture also supports the use of practical truth tests. It is only after considerable reflection that a thoughtful person realizes that knowledge requires a commitment to a worldview that is sufficient to support it. Also, such reflection makes use of the very principles it seeks to explain. In summary, epistemological self-consciousness is a process by which we *discover* the precise relationship between method and content. Most human reasoning takes place with little or no awareness of the beliefs required to account for knowledge. An important aspect of apologetics is showing that Christian theism is sufficient to meet those requirements while other worldviews fail to provide the necessary preconditions.

to synthesize Hackett's basic categories? These are only the most general questions, but they will serve well to guide the study to its intended goal.

In the interest of avoiding confusion over the key concepts, it will be helpful to clarify some important terms and explain their relevance to the study. The following four definitions are central to the main question above and to the goal of arriving at a general theory of apologetics.

Presuppositions: That which is assumed from the start of an argument operates as a presupposition. Presuppositions are at issue in apologetics because of differences concerning what is legitimately presupposed and what is not. As Aristotle aptly demonstrated, epistemological first principles are necessary to knowing anything at all.[22] In other words, knowledge requires a commitment to some principles of observation and reasoning without which meaning and reference become impossible. The larger question in apologetics is whether or not metaphysical first principles may be presupposed as necessary in the same sense as epistemological first principles. Presuppositionalists argue that they are; other apologists argue that they are not.[23]

Apologetics: Winfried Corduan offers a good working definition:

> Apologetics is the defense of Christian truth claims. It attempts to show why Christianity is intellectually acceptable. In carrying out this task, apologetic methodologies differ. Some proceed with a step-by-step verification of various Christian claims [Geisler], whereas others deal with Christianity as a whole [Van Til]. But all of these approaches have in common the goal of giving some reason for accepting the truth of Christianity.[24]

---

[22] Aristotle *Metaphysics* Bk. I: Ch. 2.

[23] I have intentionally avoided the practice of referring to all non-presuppositionalists as evidentialists. The reason for this is that the term is not sufficiently comprehensive to include all other apologists. Norman Geisler explains: "The difference between the classical apologists and the evidentialists on the use of historical evidence is that the classical see the need to first establish that this is a theistic universe in order to establish the possibility of and identity of miracles. Evidentialists do not see theism as a logically necessary precondition of historical apologetics." Geisler, "Types of Apologetics," in *Encyclopedia of Apologetics*, 42.

[24] Winfried Corduan, *Handmaid to Theology: An Essay in Philosophical Prolegomena* (Grand Rapids: Baker Books House, 1981), 16. This

Contemporary Evangelical Apologetics: The principles and methods of the Christian defense proposed by conservative Protestants since the end of World War II. The creativity and innovation of Christian apologists during this period has provided tremendous resources for clarifying major apologetic differences and providing for a more unified apologetic theory.

Synthesis: To synthesize is to combine elements into a whole. Therefore, a methodological synthesis means combining the elements of a number of methods into a single method. Methodological synthesis is not to be understood in terms of a mere apologetic eclecticism. A synthesis must provide a rationally consistent framework in which to integrate and interpret the important contributions of the main apologetic schools. The success of such a synthesis requires the discovery of shared principles undergirding all apologetic schools. A substantial unity among the schools would be demonstrated by showing that each school requires the main insights of the others in order to give an account of its own basic principles.[25] A complete synthesis is impossible since some statements in the diverse literature of apologetics are contradictory.

General Theory: A general theory is a system of ideas that includes, affects or is applicable to the issues involved in the field of apologetics. It is general in the sense that it is adequate to explain the field as a whole

---

citation references Geisler's *Christian Apologetics* and Van Til's *Defense of the Faith* as examples of different apologetic methodologies.

[25] It will be argued, for example, that epistemological and metaphysical first principles depend on each other. While many apologists acknowledge this dependence, there is disagreement as to precisely how they are related. A general theory of apologetics must explain this relationship and provide a basis to evaluate the different proposals on the question. The argument will demonstrate that each school makes a necessary contribution to this question, but no single school has integrated the contributions of the others. The goal of an apologetic synthesis is a modest one in that it incorporates the main insights of each school and attempts to adjudicate important differences. Some differences cannot be resolved by a general theory and need not be. The derivation of the categories of thought, for example, is a case in point. Are these a reflection of sensation, innate capacity, or innate ideas? The relationship of metaphysical and epistemological first principles may inform the answer to this question but does not seem to determine it. A useful general theory should map areas of agreement and disagreement by providing an underlying framework of unity.

A General Synthesis of Apologetics

while allowing for exceptions to the paradigm that do not fit neatly into the established categories. This is especially important in apologetics because individual apologists will not always fit precisely in one category or another.[26] A good general theory is able to include these exceptions, being sufficiently comprehensive to include borderline cases.

THE GUIDING ASSUMPTION

The guiding assumption of this investigation is the unity of Christian truth.[27] In any controversy related to biblical truth or its defense, we must assume that the truth is available, if only we discern the right method and understand the Bible correctly. This assumption has motivated Christians over the centuries, despite their inability to come to conclusions that are universally accepted on a variety of issues. For the Christian who accepts the Bible as God's written Word, there can be no doubt that God's mind can be known. Even where the incomprehensibility of God forces us to accept elements of mystery in God's revelation, the truth is still available to the extent of our understanding. For the Christian who places hope in the progressive illumination of the Church over time, even the unresolved controversies of history may contain the seeds of a possible resolution.

The Unification of Apologetics

In the area of apologetics, there is every reason to hope for the development of a general theory to validate and explain what has proven useful in the history of apologetics and to expose what is likely to fail. Contemporary evangelical apologists have spent as much time analyzing the approaches of the past as they have formulating their own.[28-29] Classic

---

[26] In order to synthesize the contributions of evangelical apologists, they must first be sorted out. This is where Hackett's categories are especially helpful. By sorting apologists according to presuppositional commitment, it is much easier to analyze their individual similarities and differences and to discover a way to synthesize their contributions.

[27] This assumption is based on a commitment to biblical infallibility, which implies the coherence of truth.

[28] Bernard L. Ramm, *Types of Apologetic Systems* (Wheaton: Van Kampen Press, 1953).

[29] Bernard L. Ramm, *Varieties of Christian Apologetics* (Grand Rapids: Baker Book House, 1962). This volume is a revision of *Types of Apol-*

approaches, however, are usually integrated or criticized according to the use each apologist makes of them within the parameters of his own system. No attempt has been made at a broader general theory to explain the underlying unity of the classic approaches. Indeed, the differing epistemological starting points of the classic approaches have tended to discourage the idea of a synthesis. At the very least, some theory to account for the differences is required before a synthesis can be attempted. Stuart Hackett's presuppositional analysis is certainly an excellent starting point for the required analysis, but more is needed.

Part of what is required to complete the task is a theory of philosophical disagreements that can account for both the similarities and differences evident in contemporary evangelical apologetics. W.T. Jones in a profound address to the American Philosophical Society has proposed such a theory.[30] Jones's theory is that philosophical disagreements result from differing pre-cognitive orientations. As these orientations are understood, it becomes possible to see the way to a substantial unification of apologetics. Jones provides evidence that philosophical positions are better understood as points on a continuum, rather than as isolated options.[31] If he is correct, we would expect to be able to arrive at middle ground positions that incorporate the legitimate concerns from both poles of a controversy.[32]

---

ogetic Systems, in which the author replaces the last two chapters originally dealing with Cornelius Van Til and Edward Carnell with John Calvin and Abraham Kuyper. The substitution was made in the interest of staying with the classic examples of apologetics. This decision on Ramm's part involves both a gain and a loss, as the chapters on Van Til and Carnell in the original volume are excellent summaries of these two great contemporary apologists.

[30] W.T. Jones, "Philosophical Disagreements and World Views," *Proceedings and Addresses of the American Philosophical Society* 43 (1969-70), 24-42.

[31] The idea of a theoretical continuum is what connects W.T. Jones with Stuart Hackett. Even though Hackett speaks of three categories of presuppositionalism, it is better to view these categories as three points on a continuum. Indeed, the individual differences among evangelical apologists would seem to forbid simple categorizing without allowing for degrees of difference.

[32] I recognize that this sounds very much like Hegel's dialectical approach of deriving a synthesis from a thesis and its antithesis. As it turns

In addition to differing pre-cognitive orientations, apologists also reflect differing cognitive orientations on the issue of epistemic justification. It is also necessary to deal with these differences to see if there is any way to mediate the controversy between the foundationalist and coherentist theories of epistemic justification. This debate is at the heart of evangelical apologetics and affects how apologists structure their approaches.[33] Any attempt to unify apologetics requires a response to this controversy that does justice to the concerns of each side of the debate. While some evangelicals argue for the bankruptcy of classical foundationalism,[34-35] others argue that some expression of foundationalism is inescapable.[36]

Three Basic Presuppositional Categories

In order to synthesize a general theory of apologetics from the range of contemporary evangelical options, it is more important to survey key exemplars than it is to catalogue the contributions of every notable apologist. According to Hackett's classification of apologetic systems, there are only three basic presuppositional categories that capture the entire range of argumentative apologetics.[37] Apologists have differing priorities and

---

out, it is often possible to offer a synthesis of opposing positions. No commitment to Hegel's system is implied by this similarity. What Jones really offers is a theory for use in philosophical analysis and problem solving.

[33] John Thomas Meadors, *The Foundationalist Debate and Contemporary Christian Apologetics* (Ph.D. diss., The Southern Baptist Theological Seminary, 1993).

[34] Kelly James Clark, *Return to Reason: A Critique of Enlightenment Evidentialism and a Defense of Reason and Belief in God* (Grand Rapids: Wm. B. Eerdmans Publishing Co., 1990). Clark represents Reformed epistemology and argues specifically against classical foundationalism and in favor of Reidian foundationalism.

[35] Richard R. Topping, "The Anti-Foundationalist Challenge to Evangelical Apologetics," *The Evangelical Quarterly* 63, no. 1 (1991): 45-60.

[36] Norman L. Geisler, "Foundationalism," in *Baker Encyclopedia of Christian Apologetics* (Grand Rapids: Baker Book House, 1999), 259.

[37] Like Hackett, I am not concerned to deal with non-argumentative approaches to defending the Christian faith, such as mysticism or existentialism. While Jones's theory also explains these approaches, they are

preferences in terminology.³⁸ The consistency with which an apologist follows a particular epistemology also makes a difference. Two apologists who would call themselves "Christian Rationalists" may differ on the value of sense experience in the acquisition of knowledge.³⁹ Such differences of degree illustrate that apologetic options are more like points on a continuum than discrete positions. Lines must be drawn, however, to distinguish one category from another along the continuum.

By limiting the apologists and their philosophical counterparts to two of each school, the study maintains its focus. Also, since the main purpose is to survey the apologists' and philosophers' presuppositional commitments, there is no reason to do a detailed study of the contributions of each exemplar. The analysis is meant to provide a basis to perform a methodological synthesis. The first apologist of each school was chosen as a prototype or classic example of that school. The second apologist of each school was chosen because of a creative tendency to extend the basic method to be more inclusive of insights from the school to the right, left or on both sides of the apologist.

The quest for a general theory of apologetics requires a *theoretical* approach in which the role of presuppositions in evangelical apologetics is analyzed and synthesized into a general theory. This method best serves the goal of integrating and extending the existing theory of apologetic presuppositions one step beyond its current development. By identifying the current limitations of the theory of presuppositions, it is possible to arrive at a more consistent and comprehensive theory. Developing a general theory of apologetics could seem to be an unmanageable task, making it impossible to select all of the relevant data. The value of Hack-

---

fideistic in orientation. I deal with so-called fideistic approaches in detail in my book, *Evangelical Belief: A Course Guide to Christian Thought*. An entire section of that book is devoted to the approaches of Pascal and Kierkegaard.

³⁸ In the area of hypothesis testing, for example, J. Oliver Buswell prefers the term "integration," John Warwick Montgomery uses "retroduction" and Edward J. Carnell uses "systematic consistency." All three terms have essentially the same meaning.

³⁹ A comparison of Gordon Clark with Edward Carnell illustrates this point. Clark was more consistently rationalistic than Carnell. While Clark was concerned with logical consistency, Carnell advocated "systematic consistency," which includes input from sense experience.

ett's classification scheme is that it narrows the scope of the issues for consideration and defines the relevant questions. In order to specify the priorities of the investigation, it may help to state what the study does and does not entail.

The focus of this study is *not* on what is typically referred to as Christian evidences. In my opinion, the quantity and quality of these resources is such that we can only rejoice that we have been blessed by the labors of so many great apologists. Nor is the study focused on the *application* of a general theory to specific intellectual problems and challenges. In order to restrict properly the scope of the investigation, it was necessary to focus on the key problem involved in developing a general theory of apologetics: The problem of presuppositions.

The problem with presuppositions is two-fold: (1) *What* should we assume in order to know? (2) *How* should we assume in order to know? Apologists clearly disagree on what we should assume: Should we assume "first principles" only, or must we assume a specific content or worldview? How we assume is related to what we assume: Should we hold our assumptions hypothetically or categorically? In other words, are presuppositions held experimentally or necessarily? Are they part of a thought construct or a construct of thought itself?

According to Hackett, apologists may be divided into three categories according to this problem: (1) Categorical Presuppositionalists, (2) Analytical Presuppositionalists, and (3) Metaphysical Presuppositionalists. Categorical presuppositionalists presuppose only first principles, which they hold categorically, or as necessary to knowing anything at all. Analytical Presuppositionalists also accept certain first principles as categorical presuppositions, but these are viewed as inadequate to adjudicate worldviews. In addition, one must adopt a worldview hypothetically in order to test its adequacy. Metaphysical Presuppositionalists accept Christian theism as a categorical presupposition, believing it to be absolutely necessary for the possibility of predication. The other two schools are viewed as placing the cart before the horse because they assume what can be supported only on a Christian base.

The following chart is based on Hackett's basic categories, but the layout is original with the exception of a few details adapted from the chart by Charles Horne. As a general map of the entire study, it provides the reader with a visual layout of the issues and options of argumentative apologetics as these have been developed by evangelical apologists:

Basic Categories	Categorical Presuppositionalism	Analytical Presuppositionalism	Metaphysical Presuppositionalism
Presuppositional Scope	Minimal	Moderate	Maximal
Presuppositional Function	Categorical	Hypothetical	Categorical
Presuppositional Content	First Principles	Christian Theism	Christian Theism
Presuppositional Modality	Experiential	Logical	Transcendental
Common Ground Point of Contact	Epistemological	Epistemological	Metaphysical
Method of Proof Rational Procedure	Induction Deduction	Retroduction Abduction	Transcendental Argument
Extent of Proof Degree of Certainty	Practical Certainty	Moral Certainty	Logical Certainty
Apologetic Schools Notable Apologists	Evidentialism Buswell/Geisler	Verificationalism Carnell/Ramm	Presuppositionalism Van Til/Frame
Philosophical Parameters	Empiricism Aristotle/Kant	Rationalism Augustine/Descartes	Idealism Plato/Hegel

The basic categories listed at the top of the chart (horizontal axis) reflect Hackett's terminology, and the distinction between presuppositions held categorically and hypothetically is based on his observation: This chart presents the analytical content of the study. Given the two-fold purpose of analysis and synthesis, the analysis will proceed according to the structure of the matrix above, after which a synthesis will be proposed on the basis of criticism and extension of the major concepts. The analysis will be directed toward justifying the accuracy of the presuppositional paradigm presented in the matrix, giving special attention to the apologetic and philosophic exemplars selected. If the analysis is accurate, the synthesis and its qualifications should follow naturally from the analysis.

What makes this use of Hackett's presuppositional paradigm unique is that it goes beyond mere analysis. Hackett used it for the purpose of emphasizing differences among evangelical apologists; this study brings them together. The key to this synthesis is in the relationship between categorical and hypothetical presuppositions. Evangelical apologists have traditionally held that presuppositions must be held either categorically or hypothetically. If the following study shows that the same presupposition may be or must be held both ways at different points in the analysis of worldviews, then a synthesis among the basic presuppositional categories is possible.

Chapter 2

A GENERAL SAMPLING OF APOLOGETICS I

The literature of contemporary evangelical apologetics is extensive, and many notable scholars have made helpful contributions. The main problem at this point in the study is how to sample the most important contributions. Using Hackett's categories as a guide, it is relatively easy to select the apologists whose systems will serve as benchmarks for the study. Aside from those qualifications already mentioned, four others guided the final selection: (1) Scholarly reputation based on apologetic contributions; (2) Close conformity to the distinguishing marks of one of Hackett's categories; (3) A published statement of the apologist's approach that has served to distinguish the apologist and his method among his academic peers; (4) An academic specialization in philosophy. In essence, the goal was to identify those apologists who would generally be considered the academic leaders in contemporary evangelical apologetics.[1]

Scholarly reputation and academic leadership is usually based on the publication of a major work that represents a systematic treatment of the apologist's method. While the apologists selected for this study have published more than a single work, each one has published a book that details his thinking about apologetics in a precise way. As philosophical specialists, they write with a breadth of understanding that does justice to the complexity of apologetics and its many difficult issues.

---

[1] The selections show clearly that scholarly influence, not popular influence, was the main concern. In terms of popular influence, C.S. Lewis and Francis Schaeffer would be obvious choices for consideration. The popular cast of their writings, however, makes them less useful in developing a general theory of apologetics. The more scholarly statements, some of which also have a popular appeal, are more systematic and, in some cases, more precise than the popular offerings of Lewis and Schaeffer. As it turns out, Lewis roughly follows the outline of Geisler's apologetical method, and Schaeffer resembles Carnell. For extensive treatments of Lewis and Schaeffer, the reader may consult my two books, *Evangelical Belief: A Course Guide to Christian Thought* and *Framing Francis Schaeffer: Apologetics and Personal Integrity*.

By selecting two examples from each school of apologetics, it is possible to show the range of variation possible within each perspective. Such differences are helpful in distinguishing the issues of primary and secondary importance. For example, the epistemology of Buswell is based primarily on Aristotle, while the epistemology of Geisler is based mainly on Aquinas. As it turns out, this difference will prove to be of minor significance in evaluating the overall thrust of this school of apologetics because of a more important underlying unity between Buswell and Geisler. This difference does illustrate, however, that similar apologists may receive their philosophical inspiration from different sources.

Terminology is also vitally important to these apologists, and it is at this point that their philosophical expertise becomes especially relevant. All are concerned with precision in this area, and the result is that the issues of apologetics are clearly developed within the philosophical context.[2] There is, however, tremendous similarity in meaning among evangelical apologists, despite their differences in terminology. With respect to truth tests, for example, an apologist who wants to use the established philosophical terminology might advocate coherence, correspondence, or both tests together. Another apologist might feel that the traditional terms don't carry sufficient content for the average person and will, therefore, substitute terms like "rational coherence" and "experiential relevance" for the classical terms.[3] In the interest of reducing the two standard tests to one, still another apologist will speak of "systematic consistency."[4-5]

---

[2] Some would view Van Til as an exception on this point because of the difficulty of his terminology. In fact, the difficulty of his idealistic terminology is more likely the result of a lack of familiarity on the part of his readers. Idealism fell out of favor in America after the first thirty years of the 20th Century, so the terminology has been unfamiliar to all except those well read in philosophy. Through explanation and illustration, Van Til explained this terminology, but many of his readers found it an obstacle to understanding him. To his critics, however, Van Til's terminology served to clearly indicate the philosophical context of his apologetic, making it easier to interact with the problems he raised.

[3] Stuart C. Hackett, *Oriental Philosophy: A Westerners Guide to Eastern Thought* (Madison: The University of Wisconsin Press, 1979), 6-11.

[4] This term was made popular by Carnell, who adopted it from his mentor at Boston University, Edgar Sheffield Brightman. See Carnell, *Christian Apologetics*, 56.

These examples show that a number of motives are at work when it comes to terminology. The apologist who wishes to stress a unified view of verification will gravitate toward a single term that allows for plural aspects.[6] The apologist who wishes to stress a cumulative view of verification, on the other hand, will be more interested in separate tests that witness to the same truth in relatively independent ways. The following chapters will explain these motivations in more detail, but it is necessary to call attention to them in preparing to look at some of the better examples in evangelical apologetics.[7]

A survey of apologists could begin with an exemplar from any one of Hackett's categories. Since the present purpose is to gain an appreciation of individual apologists and their contributions, the order of their consideration is not really important. It seems best, however, to begin with the categorical presuppositionalists and to finish with the metaphysical presuppositionalists, the former being the minimalists and the latter being the maximalists when it comes to presuppositional scope. This order seems to reflect the development of the presuppositional consciousness within evangelical apologetics and to best serve the purposes of the study.

---

[5] Mayers, *Both/And*, 57.

[6] The presuppositionalism of Van Til, while seeming to reject a verificational approach, also operates with a unified concept of proof. This is especially evident in his discussion of theistic proofs. Van Til says, "The true theistic proofs undertake to show that the ideas of existence (ontological proof), of cause (cosmological proof), and purpose (teleological proof) are meaningless unless they presuppose the existence of God.... The proofs of God then become witnesses of God; and witnesses of God are God witnessing to men. The theistic proofs therefore reduce to one proof, the proof which argues that unless *this* God, the God of the Bible, the ultimate being, the Creator, the controller of the universe, be presupposed as the foundation of human experience, this experience operates in a void." Cornelius Van Til, *Common Grace and Witness Bearing* (Phillipsburg: Presbyterian and Reformed Publishing Company, 1972), 190-192.

[7] Apologetic methods tend to be either atomistic or holistic in orientation in terms of their starting points. An apologist will deem it wise to begin with either the diversity of the world and our experience or with an overall perspective that gives meaning to diverse particulars. In essence, apologetics reflects the One and Many problem. A balanced approach should be *both* atomistic and holistic, uniting both the One and the Many. In fact, all apologists strive for this goal, but they differ on where to start.

In developing his apologetic categories, Hackett chose to focus on metaphysical presuppositionalists. He included Van Til, Clark, Henry and Carnell in this category. The other two categories are viewed as two complementary approaches embodied in his own apologetic. Hackett explains their relationship as follows: Categorical or experiential Presuppositionalism applies the "rational categories" to all available data, which leads to an "ultimate metaphysical principle." This procedure is similar to Analytical Presuppositionalism, which tests a theoretical system "already constructed." The difference here is that Categorical Presuppositonalism comes to the "ultimate real" through a "positive interpretation of experience" whereas Analytical Presuppositionalism is a negative procedure for testing worldviews as whole systems.[8]

Since Analytical Presuppositionalism is a *negative* method for testing worldviews, it does not provide the basis upon which to arrive at an ultimate metaphysical principle. A negative method may validate or invalidate a worldview, but it cannot establish a worldview. Categorical Presuppositionalism, as a positive method, leads to the assertion that theism is the only adequate explanation for the intelligibility of experience. But many apologists, notably Carnell, have argued that the existence of God cannot be proved in this way "since if God's existence is presupposed in any order of intelligibility, then such existence cannot be argued on the basis of such intelligibility."[9] In short, if one must presuppose God to explain experience, one cannot prove God from experience. In Carnell's words, "God gets in the way of all demonstration of deity, for His existence is the *sin qua non* for all demonstration."[10] Hackett responds to this objection as follows:

> But this is indeed a strange objection: it is quite true that, if theism be correct, then the existence of God is metaphysically basic to all rational structure. *But the individual does not start with this knowledge when he approaches experience—it is the fact of God's existence, not the knowledge of it, which makes rational structure, whether in argument or reality, possible. And it is the very showing that the rationality of existence presupposes*

---

[8] Hackett, *Resurrection of Theism*, 156-157.

[9] Ibid., 157.

[10] Ibid.

God that constitutes the demonstration of His existence. Proof for God is possible just because all men start with a rational experience which, if rationally interpreted leads to the conclusion that God exists.[11] (emphasis mine)

For Hackett, knowledge does not require the *presupposition* of God; rather, it requires the *existence* of God. Knowledge is possible *because* God exists, not because we *know* he exists from the start of the thinking process. God becomes an *implication* of rational experience, not the *presupposition* of such experience.[12] These aspects of Hackett's thinking are necessary to understanding his presuppositional categories; his own apologetic method closely resembles Geisler's Thomistic approach, although Hackett is inspired more by Kant than Aquinas.[13] For now, it is

---

[11] Ibid.

[12] Hackett's point here is profoundly important to understanding the different senses in which apologists speak of God's existence as rationally necessary to knowledge. He distinguishes fact and presupposition here in order to distinguish ontological necessity from epistemic necessity. Provided the distinction between the ontological and the epistemic is observed, it is possible to speak of presupposing God's existence even from Hackett's point of view. For Him, God is the ontological presupposition, not the epistemic presupposition, of knowledge. This distinction is what separates categorical presuppositionalists from analytical and metaphysical presuppositionalists. To Hackett's credit, he is the only apologist encountered through this study who stresses this point. In doing so, he has uncovered a major source of confusion within evangelical apologetics with respect to presuppositions.

[13] Hackett's devotion to Kant's approach to synthetic *a priori* truths could seem to set him off from Geisler in a significant way. In fact, Hackett himself did not see his own approach as significantly different from others who adopted the views of Aristotle or Aquinas on the categories: "Pure rationalism would be false if there were any synthetic *a posteriori* judgments that constituted genuine knowledge; and pure empiricism would be false if there were any synthetic *a priori* truths, i.e., any truths that were logically independent of empirical experience and yet also non-definitional in nature. This 'third way' of epistemology has seemed eminently plausible to many traditional philosophers. Perhaps the most important historically was Immanuel Kant; but in my opinion, although they did not use our type of terminology, both Aristotle and Thomas Aquinas held substantially this moderate position in epistemology, although each stated the view in his own way and both have sometimes been

enough to understand why he places different apologists in the categories he does.

An obvious discrepancy between Hackett's classification and its adaptation to this study is evident with respect to Carnell. Hackett classifies him as a metaphysical presuppositionalist, whereas he is classified as an analytical presuppositionalist throughout this investigation. How can this deviation be justified? For Hackett, there are really only two types of apologists: Those who start with epistemological first principles and those who start with metaphysical first principles. Despite the fact that Carnell presupposes Christian theism in a different way than Van Til does, he nevertheless begins with a metaphysical presupposition. For this reason, Hackett classifies him with Van Til.

From another point of view, however, it is possible to distinguish apologists according to the manner in which they hold metaphysical presuppositions. Since Carnell presupposes Christian theism hypothetically and not categorically, as Van Til does, it also makes sense to distinguish him from Metaphysical Presuppositionalism. This is, in fact, what Charles Horne does.[14] By stressing the uniqueness of Van Til's position, Horne classifies any apologist who does not accept the Christian worldview "unquestioningly" as either an analytical or a categorical presuppositionalist.[15] Thus, Analytical Presuppositionalism is something of a wild card in the apologist's hand. If this presuppositional category is viewed merely as a negative test, as Hackett does, then it will not be viewed as a distinctive method in its own right. If, on the other hand, the stress is placed on the manner in which presuppositions are held, shifting the classifications of different apologists logically follows.

Both of these perspectives are valid from a certain point of view. For the purposes of this study, Horne's perspective seems more useful for analyzing evangelical apologetics. Hackett's perspective clearly distin-

---

claimed as empiricists by that tradition." Hackett, *The Reconstruction of the Christian Revelation Claim*, 21-22.

[14] Horne, Van Til and Carnell—Part II, 369. Horne places Ramm, Clark and Buswell in the analytical category along with Carnell. Contrary to Horne, this study leads to the conclusion that Buswell would be better classified with Hackett as an apologist who attempts to begin with an epistemology.

[15] Ibid., 379.

guishes his own apologetic program from that of other apologists. But in doing so, he does not stress the very important ways in which Carnell differs from Van Til. Given the method of classification used in this study, Hackett would be viewed as sharing some aspects of Analytical Presuppositionalism, just as Carnell and Clark share some aspects of Metaphysical Presuppositionalism. Hopefully, this approach will serve best to preserve the distinctiveness of the apologists and to illustrate the lines of continuity among them.

TWO CATEGORICAL PRESUPPOSITIONALISTS

J. Oliver Buswell and Norman Geisler have distinguished themselves as empirical apologists who attempt to develop the Christian defense from an epistemology of first principles. The late J. Oliver Buswell, Jr. was Dean Emeritus of Covenant Theological Seminary in Saint Louis, Missouri. Norman Geisler is the Distinguished Professor of Apologetics at Veritas Evangelical Seminary in Murrieta, California. Both apologists have distinguished themselves among evangelicals as leaders in the defense of evidentialism and classical apologetics respectively.[16] Buswell was best known for his *Systematic Theology* and a work on Christian philosophy that explains the basis of his apologetics.[17-18] Geisler has built his reputation on the exceptional volume, clarity, and scholarship of his contributions.

J. Oliver Buswell

Any attempt to cover the range of argumentative apologetics requires the inclusion of a major evidential apologist. In terms of scholarly reputation,

---

[16] John Gerstner and R.C. Sproul should also be mentioned as prominent advocates of classical apologetics. In terms of the popular defense of the traditional approach to apologetics, their work has had a marked impact on Evangelicalism. See R.C. Sproul, John Gerstner, and Arthur Lindsley, *Classical Apologetics: A Rational Defense of the Christian Faith and a Critique of Presuppositional Apologetics* (Grand Rapids: Zondervan Publishing House, 1984).

[17] James Oliver Buswell, Jr., *A Systematic Theology of the Christian Religion* (Grand Rapids: Zondervan Publishing House, 1962).

[18] James Oliver Buswell, Jr., *A Christian View of Being and Knowing* (Grand Rapids: Zondervan Publishing House, 1960).

Buswell is arguably the academic leader among contemporary evangelical evidentialists. While other notable examples might serve the purposes of the study equally well, Buswell came before them with a focused philosophical defense of evidentialism.[19] The breadth of his scholarship is evident in his *Systematic Theology*, which is a fresh and creative statement of evangelical Reformed theology.[20]

Gordon Lewis describes Buswell's approach as "pure empiricism" because it allows for "no unexamined presuppositions."[21] Unlike Clark and Van Til, Buswell appealed to evidence that would be persuasive to believers and non-Christians. Unlike Hackett and Hamilton, Buswell considered no presuppositions or logical principles as innate to the mind or self-attesting. Lewis also claims that Buswell accepted John Locke's view that the mind—prior to experience and reflection—is a blank tablet, a *tabula rasa*: "All ideas arise by reflection upon experience.... For him *all* knowledge is rooted in experience *alone*."[22]

---

[19] The extremely valuable work of Dr. John Warwick Montgomery has had a popular impact that goes beyond that of Buswell. Montgomery has been concerned to develop the historical and juridical aspects of evidentialism. He has also stressed an application of his approach to the "tender-minded," those who require a defense of Christianity that is not centered primarily on rational argumentation. The breadth of Montgomery's apologetical concerns and the creativity of his scholarly offerings has inspired many popular evidentialists, such as Josh McDowell and David Noebel.

[20] This work deserves a great deal more attention than it has received. Buswell was an excellent theological writer, and he offers creative perspectives on the doctrines of God and eschatology. While retaining great respect for prominent theologians of the Reformed tradition, such as Machen and Hodge, the influence of Evangelicalism is also evident in this work, especially in the section on eschatology. The last section of the work is a defense of mid-tribulational premillenialism, complete with a commentary of the book of Revelation. In a personal conversation with Dr. Gordon Lewis, a former student of Buswell, Lewis recalled to me that his teacher was an eccentric lecturer with an exceptional knowledge of the original languages of the Bible. Buswell would sometimes roam the streets of New York City, where he was a minister from 1922 to 1926, reading from his Greek New Testament.

[21] Gordon R. Lewis, *Testing Christianity's Truth Claims: Approaches to Christian Apologetics* (Chicago: Moody Press, 1976), 46.

[22] Ibid., 46-47.

In understanding Buswell, it is important to remember that he did believe in the use of presuppositions. The fact that presuppositions must be tested does not mean that they do not have a role to play once they are verified. Also, Buswell's empiricism should not be understood to exclude *a priori* truths. His own writings verify that, like Aristotle and Aquinas, Buswell believed that knowledge does involve what is prior to experience. The *a priori*, however, is ontological, not epistemological. In other words, what is prior is *discovered* in experience, not brought to it, as in rationalism.

The appeal of empiricism is best understood over against the problems of modern philosophy. Mortimer Adler explains:

> John Locke espoused a view of the human mind that had been held by almost all his predecessors in antiquity and the Middle Ages. That view regarded the human mind as a tabula rasa, a blank but impressionable tablet. The opposition view, introduced by Immanuel Kant, attributed to the human mind an innate structure, prior to all experience—forms of intuition and categories of the understanding—that shaped experience so definitely that our mind-determined experience, in effect, became an obstacle to our knowing the reality of things in themselves. Only if the other view is correct, the view that the mind has no innate perceptual forms and no innate conceptual categories, can it be true that our mind-dependent experience does not preclude us from having knowledge of reality—of things in themselves—through that experience. What William James, in *Pragmatism*, called our commonsense categories were not like Kant's transcendental categories.[23]

The appeal of empiricism is based on the need for objectivity. The Kantian program becomes an "obstacle" to knowing reality because our experience is always tainted by the mind, which filters our experience through the categories. Since the categories are not discovered through experience but are considered epistemological givens, we cannot know whether the structure of the world matches the categories or is created by them. Hence, Kant logically drew the conclusion that things in themselves cannot be known.

---

[23] Mortimer Adler, *Intellect: Mind Over Matter* (New York: Macmillan Publishing Company, 1990), 116.

Empiricism itself, however, seems to be faced with a similar problem because of the idea that all knowledge is derived from experience. Carnell contended that knowledge can never attain a universal and necessary status on the basis of sense perceptions alone, "for from flux only flux can come." The senses merely report a succession of disjointed impressions (Hume) and therefore demonstrate nothing absolutely.[24]

Hackett adds to Carnell's criticism of empiricism by pointing out that the categories are really added to experience, not derived from it: "*Every attempt to derive the categories from the data of experience presupposes their use in the attempted derivation.*" In other words, the category of causation is not derived from experience but brought to it. Empiricism, then, puts the cart before the horse by not recognizing that the categorical structure of human thought is what makes experience possible. So the categories are the precondition—not the product—of thought.[25]

Among the criticisms of empiricism, these two get to the heart of the issue and show why a number of prominent evangelical apologists reject evidentialism from the start. It is probably safe to say that a crass sensationalism as a basis for apologetics is refuted on the basis of these two problems. But is this what Buswell is advocating? As it turns out, Buswell offers a response to these problems. He clearly understood them, giving a clear answer to the question of "the source or ground of the laws of reason." These are not merely "self-evident" in the sense that they "contain their own verification." Nor are they "innate ideas" as the rationalists affirmed. In fact, the laws of reason do *not* have an empirical basis but are "derived from the character of God." Since it is impossible for God to lie, we may count on the coherence, correspondence, and integration of God's word with the created reality of our experience. The laws of reason, therefore, are based on the character of God and are accepted on the basis of all those reasons we accept the Christian worldview. This means that the laws of reason are not produced by a process of inquiry (Dewey) but are "discoverable" by experience, which includes divine revelation and its evidences: "I believe, as Peirce believed, that the laws of reason are eternal verities, but that they are *discovered* empirically."[26]

---

[24] Carnell, *Christian Apologetics*, 129.

[25] Hackett, *Resurrection of Theism*, 62-63.

[26] Buswell, *Being and Knowing*, 193-194.

This answer is the key to understanding both Buswell and evidential apologetics. The laws of logic are "obtained by and in the process of experience." In short, they are *a priori* and "eternal verities" discovered empirically. But what about Carnell's criticism that empirical knowledge "can never rise to the universal and necessary, for from flux only flux can come"? In answer to this question, Buswell offers his entire apologetic, "all the reasons for my acceptance of the Christian system of doctrine and life." The consistency, coherence, correspondence and integration with ontological reality of whatever God has said ultimately supports belief in *a priori* truths. Nor is faith excluded, for *faith in reason* is necessary to philosophical understanding. Faith is the "volitional element" in understanding, the willingness to commit to the reliability of reason.[27]

The emphasis on faith in reason implies Buswell's awareness that ultimately neither reason nor sense experience has the power to compel belief. It is possible to say no to both. This is important in the debate over certainty. Doubt and unbelief are always possible, no matter what kind of argument is put forth. One may doubt a logically certain argument just as easily as one may doubt a highly probable one because faith in the criteria used to build an argument is always in question.[28] In this respect, Buswell affirms the Augustinian principle, *credo ut intelligam*: I believe that I may understand.

How, then, do presuppositions function in this apologetic? In fact, they play a major role, but not as the epistemic starting points of the Christian defense. Christian theism is first established through the theistic

---

[27] Ibid., 198.

[28] The profound importance of this point is often unrecognized by apologists in discussing the criteria used in justifying belief. The diatribe against probability usually overlooks the equally valid diatribe against formality. Arguments for Christian theism purporting logical certainty allow for doubts concerning the correspondence between the substance of the argument and the real world. An argument that structures the world is, in its own way, no stronger than an argument from the structure of the world, and for some it is considered much weaker. There are many for whom the witness of experience is much more compelling than the witness of rationality. This is especially true in times when scientific confidence is high and philosophic confidence is low. The multiplicity of different religious and philosophical worldviews leads many to the modest orientation of an evidentialism like Buswell's.

proofs reformulated along inductive lines.[29] Then the Bible is established as the word of God through the use of traditional Christian evidences. This method proceeds according to the criteria mentioned above: Coherence, correspondence, and the integration of the Christian system of truth.

Buswell says that the primary presupposition of the Christian religion is Jesus Christ: "It is rather, *Jesus Christ as the Second Person of the sovereign Triune Godhead, as presented in the Bible, His infallible Word*, which constitutes our one complex primary presupposition."[30] This presupposition, however, is "a conclusion arrived at on the basis of what we consider good and sufficient reasons."[31] The Christian must always be ready to state the reasons for this presupposition for the purposes of clarifying and confirming the Christian faith and for convincing non-Christians. As a *conclusion*, the Christian presupposition is arrived at on the basis of an inductive method, the laws of logic, the testimony of the Holy Spirit, and the integration of the Christian system.

The laws of logic are accepted for three reasons: (1) All discourse comes to an end without them, (2) They are backed by "good experimental evidence," and (3) They are "implicit if not explicit" in the Scriptures.[32] The processes of inductive reasoning are also assumed:

> We shall argue that God is known by his effects, that is by revelation, in Christ, in Scripture, and in His creation, when we present the theistic proofs. Inductive reasoning in theology carries us as far, and is as reliable, as inductive reasoning is, or claims to be in any sphere.[33]

The limitations of induction, however, require something more for Christian certainty. The work of the Holy Spirit is also essential:

> Similarly the Christian theologian is sufficiently familiar with the Word of God, and with the promptings of the Holy Spirit, to believe whatever Jesus said because He said it, even though none of us have completely verified all His sayings by the experimental method. We not only believe

---

[29] Buswell, *Systematic Theology*, 72-101.

[30] Ibid., 15.

[31] Ibid.

[32] Ibid, 21.

[33] Ibid., 23.

the evidence, we believe Him. *The work of the Holy Spirit in bringing conviction to the hearts of men is above and beyond the inductive rational process, but never contrary thereto.*[34] (emphasis mine)

The integration of the Christian system is not only an evidence for its truth, but it is also a key to apologetic strategy. Because every doctrine implies the others, the statement and defense of the Christian faith may begin anywhere: "The question is not where must we necessarily begin by force of logic, but where is it practical to begin?"[35] While a defense of theism using the theistic proofs is often the best place to begin, it is not a necessary starting point. This aspect of Buswell's approach is important because it directly contradicts the Thomistic strategy of Norman Geisler, who argues that the proof for theism necessarily comes before Christian evidences.

Some apologists would argue that Buswell's notion that presuppositions are conclusions represents a misuse of the term. There is, however, a profoundly biblical insight behind his approach. The Christian's complex presupposition does function as such in reasoning about matters that go beyond sense experience. In fact, Hebrews 11:1 supports Buswell's understanding: "Now faith is being sure of what we hope for and certain of what we do not see." The word translated *certain* in the NIV signifies a *proof* or *test* of unseen things.[36] The Christian presupposition, which is the objec-

---

[34] Ibid.

[35] Ibid., 26.

[36] "There is a further ambiguity about the word translated 'certain' (GK 1793), which usually signifies a 'proof' or 'test.' Some take it here as 'test' and some see its legal use, while many prefer to understand it in much the same sense as the preceding expression (e.g., NIV). If we were to adopt the meaning 'test,' then the author is saying that faith, in addition to being the basis of all that we hope for, is that by which we test things unseen. We have no material way of assessing the significance of the immaterial. But Christians are not helpless. We have faith and by this we test all things. 'What we do not see' excludes the entire range of visible phenomena which here stand for all things earthly. Faith extends beyond what we learn from our senses. Its tests are not those of the senses, which yield uncertainty." Kenneth L. Barker and John R. Kohlenberger III, eds., *NIV Bible Commentary: Volume 2: New Testament* (Grand Rapids: Zondervan Publishing House, 1994), 993.

tive expression of the Christian's faith ("the substance of things hoped for" KJV), becomes the test by which metaphysical propositions are proved.[37] In actuality, Buswell's concept of presuppositions is on solid biblical ground, even if it seems unusual from a philosophic and apologetic point of view.[38]

Norman Geisler

Van Til has described the methodology of Norman Geisler and other classical apologists as a "block house" methodology. Unlike Van Til's method of defending Christian theism as a unit, the classical method deals "with theism first and then Christianity afterwards."[39] According to Geisler, there are two main reasons for this approach. First, one cannot defend a supernatural worldview, such as Christianity, unless a God exists to account for the supernatural elements. Miracles, for example, have a different interpretation within an atheistic universe than they do within a theistic universe. Hence, it is necessary to prove the existence of God in order to make Christianity intelligible. Second, the proof for theism and the evidence for Christianity ought to be based on criteria that do not epistemologically depend on the acceptance of Christianity or theism from the outset. If the existence of God can be demonstrated on the basis of first principles, which cannot be reasonably denied by any thinking person, then belief in God cannot be rejected as circular reasoning or begging the question.

The first point above is explained by Geisler over against evidentialism, which is understood to include the idea that meaning arises directly

---

[37] See Buswell, *Systematic Theology*, II:185-186, which shows that Buswell himself embraced this interpretation of Hebrews 11:1.

[38] See Francis A. Schaeffer, "A Review of a Review," in *The Bible Today*, May (1948), 7-9. In this review article, Schaeffer attempts to harmonize the main concerns of both Buswell and Van Til. At different points, Schaeffer approvingly quotes Buswell on the use of hypothetical reasoning and inductive evidences. Some confusion concerning Francis Schaeffer's use of the term *presupposition* could have been avoided if his interpreters had recognized that he was following Buswell on this point and not Van Til. Buswell heavily influenced Schaeffer. Schaeffer often uses Buswell's phrase, *good and sufficient reasons*, when referring to the support for Christian presuppositions.

[39] Van Til, *Defense of the Faith*, 132.

from facts. Given the distinction between facts and their interpretation, meaning always requires a context or framework to make the facts intelligible. For example, a miracle like the resurrection makes sense within the framework of a supernatural worldview like Christianity, but not in the context of a naturalistic worldview. As Geisler puts it, "No bare fact possesses inherent meaning; every fact is an 'interprefact' by virtue of a necessary combination of both its bare facticity and the meaning given to it in a given context by a specific perspective or world view."[40]

In the case of Christian miracles, the evidentialist might respond that the context of a miraculous event is provided by the Bible itself. The words of Christ concerning his miracles and the prophetic words of the Old Testament supply the necessary correlation between word and fact. To this Geisler responds that facts—by themselves—provide no basis to identify some facts as special or as having "ultimate significance." The mental process of selecting and comparing brings "principles or perspectives" to the facts that do not arise from the facts themselves. A series of atypical events that would be viewed as miraculous in a theistic universe would be viewed as freak events in a random universe. Therefore, the miracles and prophesies appealed to by Christians require a Christian theistic context for their meaning.[41]

According to Geisler, when the evidentialist appeals to miracles or prophecy or the correlation between the two as evidence for the existence of God and the truth of Christianity, he "begs the whole question."[42] Unless it is first proved that God exists, these unusual occurrences are merely "an odd series of combinations."[43] Of course, the evidentialist may still respond that the odds of such combinations may be studied in relationship to the usual course of events and shown to be so astronomically unlikely as to justify our taking them as genuinely miraculous. A true evidentialist would not come to the facts with the presupposition of a "random universe" simply because the world of our experience does not support the idea that the world is random. Because of the integration of Christian theism, the evidentialist may begin with any fact; the theistic context emerges from an inductive consideration of the facts taken in any order.

---

[40] Geisler, *Christian Apologetics*, 96.

[41] Ibid., 96-97.

[42] Ibid., 97.

[43] Ibid.

For Geisler, the establishment of theism requires an assessment of the methodologies commonly used to establish the truth: Agnosticism, Rationalism, Fideism, Experientialism, Evidentialism, Pragmatism, and Combinationalism. Five major worldviews have resulted from the application of these methods: Deism, Pantheism, Panentheism, Atheism, and Theism. These five worldviews represent the "limited number of mutually exclusive ways to view the whole of reality."[44] In examining philosophical methods and their worldview products, Geisler intends "to show that all the major alternative worldviews are self-defeating and inadequate and that only theism stands the test for truth" that Geisler proposes.[45]

The different methods or truth tests commonly used to justify worldviews fail for various reasons. After summarizing each test and its major proponents, Geisler concludes that all six tests are inadequate. Rationalism fails because all rational justification must come to an end in first principles, and these cannot be used as a basis for proving logic without arguing in a circle. Furthermore, even granting the validity of the laws of thought, "they cannot be validly used to demonstrate any reality by logical necessity."[46] At best, logical consistency serves as a negative test for truth, since the consistency of any system of belief does not prove its truth. In practice, the rationalist would have to be omniscient in order to know which systems are ultimately consistent and which are ultimately contradictory.

Fideism is not even a test for truth, according to Geisler, but simply a claim for truth. To be consistent, the fideist cannot appeal to any other belief as a ground for his ultimate belief, for to do so is to be fideistic in his *claim* for truth while employing a rational or pragmatic *test* for truth. "Beliefs alone are not self-justifying; they are only claims that call for confirmation outside themselves."[47] Experience is also not self-justifying or self-interpreting. Experience requires a framework or mold to give shape and meaning to the "stuff" of experience. "Truth is propositional; it is an expression about experience," and different molds may be used to

---

[44] Ibid., 151.

[45] Ibid.

[46] Ibid., 137.

[47] Ibid., 138.

shape the "Jello" of experience.[48] Thus, experientialism fails for the same reasons as fideism.

Evidentialism fails for reasons already mentioned. Like experientialism, evidentialism is inadequate because facts are not self-interpreting. "Hence, bare facts as such cannot establish the truth of a model, and facts as interpreted by a model cannot be used to establish the truth of the model which provides the justification for interpreting the facts in that particular way."[49]

The combinational test combines two or more of the previous tests and is sometimes referred to as "systematic consistency." "Often it entails three tests: logical consistency, empirical adequacy, and experiential relevance. Whatever the form, combinationalism is also insufficient as a test for the truth of a worldview because it does not eliminate the possibility of other views being true."[50] Geisler accounts for this weakness in terms of the Leaky Bucket fallacy. By combining a series of inadequate tests or leaky buckets, one does not come up with an adequate test for truth. If rationalism or evidentialism alone fails to hold water, then how will the two buckets together hold more water than a single leaky bucket?[51]

What then does Geisler propose as an adequate test for truth? "We propose that *undeniability* is the test for the truth of a world view and *unaffirmability* is the test for the falsity of a world view."[52] Put simply, an unaffirmable statement is *sayable* but self-defeating, which means that what is affirmed is denied in the very act of affirmation. A statement is directly unaffirmable "when the statement itself provides the information to defeat itself," such as "I cannot express myself in words." A statement is indirectly unaffirmable if the *process* by which a conclusion is derived contradicts the thought expressed in the statement. Geisler uses agnosticism as an example of an indirectly self-defeating assertion: "I know that one cannot know anything about reality" implies that the agnostic knows enough about reality to know what cannot be known about it. Unless the

---

[48] Ibid.

[49] Ibid., 139.

[50] Ibid., 140.

[51] Ibid.

[52] Ibid., 141.

statement is false, the agnostic has no *basis* upon which to make the statement.53

If what is unaffirmable is false, then what is undeniable is presumably true. Just as statements may be unaffirmable in two ways, so a position may be undeniable in two ways. Definitional undeniability refers to statements that are undeniably true by definition, such as "triangles must have three sides." God might also be understood to be definitionally undeniable if he is a necessary Being. The problem with definitions of God and triangles is that neither guarantees the *existence* of that to which they refer. In the end, such definitions "are purely mathematical or theoretical. As such, they are empty tautologies, and no tautology or definitional statement tells us anything about the real world."54

Existential undeniability may be claimed for certain statements, the denial of which leads to a contradiction. For example, I cannot deny my own existence without existing. At this point, Geisler makes an important qualification that must be observed lest too much be claimed on the basis of existential undeniability. The claim that I *must* exist in order to deny my own existence does not carry the idea of *logical necessity*. Since my existence is not logically necessary, for I might not exist, my existence is only necessary to make statements like "I think therefore I am." In short, "existential truth cannot be legislated; it must be looked for in experience." If something is definitionally undeniable, then it must be found to be actually undeniable; existence can never be assumed on the basis of definitions.55

Armed with these truth tests, Geisler goes on to show "that all non-theistic worldviews are directly or indirectly unaffirmable and only theism is affirmable and, hence, only theism is true."56 But what about *Christian* theism? The traditional truth tests, while inadequate to adjudicate among worldviews, are adequate for judging claims *within* a given worldview. Combinationalism, or systematic coherence, in particular seems to be the best test for truth. Geisler faces an important question at this point because of his previous rejection of combinationalism: How do "leaky buck-

---

[53] Ibid., 142.

[54] Ibid., 143.

[55] Ibid., 144.

[56] Ibid., 145.

et" arguments serve Christian theism if they were of no use in making the theistic argument?[57] Geisler's answer is consistent with his overall epistemology: A combinational approach may not work in judging among worldviews, but it is useful once the correct worldview is established. In other words, a number of different worldviews might all be systematically consistent, which means that systematic consistency is powerless to identify the correct worldview. But in judging different versions of Theism, for example, this test provides the only way to determine which version is internally consistent and "factually all-inclusive": "In short, *all* the facts interpreted in an internally consistent way are a sufficient test for truth within a given metaphysical system."[58]

In essence, arguments that are leaky buckets when attempting to judge *among* worldviews become sound when adjudicating claims *within* an established worldview. "Or, to state it another way, once a macromodel is established for interpreting all the experiences and occurrences in the world, then the most consistent and comprehensive way the micromodels are fitted into it is the indication of truth."[59] Even used properly, however, systematic consistency does not provide an "apodictic or undeniable test for truth." Finite minds are incapable of fully comprehending all the relationships between facts, so probability is the guide. In summary, theism is undeniable and Christian theism is probable: "If Christianity

---

[57] See Anthony Flew, *An Introduction to Western Philosophy: Ideas and Argument from Plato to Popper* (New York: Thames and Hudson, 1989), 287. Flew's comments on this fallacy in relation to Descartes' argument for the existence of God are important: "Yet the whole performance may seem to some an application of the Ten-leaky-buckets Tactic—presenting a series of generally unsound arguments as if their mere conjunction might render them collectively valid: something which needs to be distinguished carefully from the accumulation of evidence, where every item possesses some weight in its own right." Clearly, the leaky buckets fallacy is not committed where every item of argument possesses some weight in its own right. Especially pregnant are Flew's words, "may seem to some." Whether a set of arguments constitutes bona fide evidence or a set of leaky buckets is frequently based more on individual bias than fair philosophical assessment. One might fault Geisler's previous rejection of combinationalism as a worldview test for truth as an unjustified application of the leaky buckets fallacy to worthy evidences used in combination.

[58] Geisler, *Christian Apologetics*, 145-146.

[59] Ibid., 146.

best explains all the known facts in the most consistent way, then it should be accepted as truth."[60]

The undeniability of theism is based on the application of undeniable epistemological first principles.[61] While Geisler has written at great length to develop his argument for the existence of God,[62] he has also provided a relatively concise version in an excellent article on first principles in his *Encyclopedia of Christian Apologetics*.[63] While the specifics of his argument for the existence of God are not of primary importance to the study, his use of first principles in developing the argument is directly relevant. The advantage of consulting his article on first principles is that it is meant to show the relationship between the statement and defense of first principles and the argument for the existence of God.

Geisler sets forth twelve basic first principles upon which everything we know about reality is built. These begin with the principles of being since, for the realist, being is the basis of knowing; "they relate thought and thing."[64]

1. Being Is = The Principle of Existence.
2. Being Is Being = The Principle of Identity.
3. Being Is Not Nonbeing = The Principle of Noncontradiction.
4. Either Being or Nonbeing = The Principle of the Excluded Middle.

---

[60] Ibid., 147.

[61] "To say that logic does not apply to reality, you have to make a logical statement about it. But if it takes a logical statement to deny logic, then your actions defeat the purpose of your words. Either way, logic must apply to reality. And if logic applies to reality, then we can use it to test truth claims about reality." Norman L. Geisler and Ron M. Brooks, *When Skeptics Ask* (Wheaton: Scripture Press Publications, Inc., 1990), 271.

[62] Norman L. Geisler, *Philosophy of Religion* (Grand Rapids: Zondervan Publishing House, 1974).

[63] Geisler, "First Principles," in *Baker Encyclopedia of Christian Apologetics*, 250-253.

[64] Ibid., 253.

5. Nonbeing Cannot Cause Being = *The Principle of Causality*.
6. Contingent Being Cannot Cause Contingent Being = *The Principle of Contingency* (or Dependency).
7. Only Necessary Being Can Cause Contingent Being = *The Positive Principle of Modality*.
8. Necessary Being Cannot Cause a Necessary Being = *The Negative Principle of Modality*.
9. Every Contingent Being is Caused by a Necessary Being = *The Principle of Existential Causality*.
10. Necessary Being Exists = The Principle of Existential Necessity.
11. Contingent Being Exists = Principle of Existential Contingency.
12. Necessary Being is similar to similar contingent being(s) it causes = *The Principle of Analogy*.[65]

While most of these principles seem obvious, they require some explanation. Some skeptics or agnostics would reject the undeniability of some of these principles, so it is necessary to defend them against those who attempt to deny the undeniable. The principle of existence (1) is undeniable because I must exist in order to deny my existence. In essence, it is undeniable because the contrary is "actually unaffirmable." The principle of identity (2) seems the most obvious since, if a thing were not identical to itself, it would not be itself.

The principles of noncontradiction (3) and excluded middle (4) are undeniable because being and nonbeing are opposites. Since opposites cannot be the same (3), nothing can exist in between being and nonbeing (4). The principle of causality (5) cannot be denied unless something can come from nothing. Stated another way, if the cause and effect relationship is denied, then what exists must have come from nothing, which is absurd. Since absolutely nothing cannot cause something (5), then neither can one contingent mode of being cause another contingent being (6). The reason for this is obvious: What cannot account for its own being cannot account for the being of another. Given principles five and six, it is unde-

---

[65] Ibid., 250.

niable that "if anything comes to be, it must be caused by a Necessary Being" (7).[66]

A Necessary Being must exist by definition (8). A necessary mode of existence excludes being caused or coming to be, "for what comes to be is not necessary."[67] All contingent beings, on the other hand, need a cause (9), since they have no basis in themselves to account for their existence (6). Since something does exist (1), then something necessarily exists (10). But since change is real, it is evident that contingent being(s) also exist (11). In other words, "not everything that exists is necessary."[68] Finally, since Necessary Being is the cause of contingent being, there must be an analogy or likeness between the two modes of being (12). "The cause of being cannot produce what it does not possess," so "the effect must resemble its cause in its being," but "it must also be different from it in its potentiality. For the cause (a Necessary Being), by its very nature, has no potential not to be."[69]

On the basis of these first principles, Geisler constructs a demonstrative proof for the existence of God:

1. Something exists (e.g., I do) (no. 1).
2. I am a contingent being (no. 11).
3. Nothing cannot cause something (no. 5).
4. Only a Necessary Being can cause a contingent being (no. 7).
5. Therefore, I am caused to exist by a Necessary Being (follows from nos. 1-4).
6. But I am a personal, rational, and moral kind of being (since I engage in these kinds of activities).
7. Therefore, this Necessary Being must be a personal rational, and moral kind of being, since I am similar to him by the principle of Analogy (no. 12).

---

[66] Ibid., 251.

[67] Ibid., 252.

[68] Ibid.

[69] Ibid., 253.

8. But a Necessary Being cannot be contingent (i.e., not-necessary) in its being which would be a contradiction (no. 3).
9. Therefore, this Necessary Being is personal, rational, and moral in a necessary way, not in a contingent way.
10. This Necessary Being is also eternal, uncaused, unchanging, unlimited, and one, since a Necessary Being cannot come to be, be caused by another, undergo change, be limited by any possibility of what it could be (a Necessary Being has no possibility to be other than it is), or to be more than one Being (since there cannot be two infinite beings).
11. Therefore, one necessary, eternal, uncaused, unlimited (=infinite), rational, personal, and moral being exists.
12. Such a Being is appropriately called "God" in the theistic sense because he possesses all the essential characteristics of a theistic God.[70]

This argument clearly shows the relationship between the use of epistemological first principles and the conclusion that God exists. By starting with first principles and the acknowledgment that something exists, a personal God is required to account for this. Winfried Corduan has presented a version of this cosmological argument using transcendental logic.[71] The advantage of a transcendental argument is that it makes more explicit the claim that God is required to account for the world.[72] This

---

[70] Ibid.

[71] "Transcendental logic is the type of reasoning process whereby we uncover necessary conditions without which certain phenomena could not be true." Corduan, *Reasonable Faith*, 108.

[72] It is important to demonstrate at the outset that transcendental arguments are not the exclusive property of metaphysical presuppositionalists like Van Til and Frame. The sense in which God is required, however, is ontological, not epistemological. Corduan does not start with the epistemic assumption that God exists and then build his argument from God as his first premise. Rather, he starts with the world and then shows that God is ontologically necessary to account for it. In this sense, classical apologists may speak of God as a necessary presupposition. On the basis of Corduan's use of transcendental logic, one may also offer a transcen-

method of inference is also more flexible because it is "not confined to the rigors of pure deductive or pure inductive argumentation."[73] As Corduan explains it, "We may not violate the laws of logic, but we do not need to follow the formal rules of argumentation, just as we do not do so in everyday life."[74] At bottom, the following argument is simply a transcendental version of Geisler's argument above:

1. Something exists.
2. Each thing that exists is either necessary or contingent.
3. A necessary being would have to be God.
4. The world cannot be a necessary being.
5. There can only be one necessary being.
6. Unless there is a necessary being there cannot be any contingent beings.
7. A necessary being exists.
8. Therefore, God exists.
9. Therefore, only one God exists.
10. The God of theism exists.[75]

Premise six is the key premise because it begins with "unless" and shows that contingent beings cannot exist *unless* there is a necessary being. This premise is at the heart of all cosmological reasoning, and it is undeniably supported by the use of epistemological first principles.

---

dental argument for the Trinity. See Schaeffer, *Trilogy*, 287-289; Frame, *Apologetics to the Glory of God*, 46-50.

[73] Ibid.

[74] Ibid.

[75] Ibid., 109.

CHAPTER 3

A GENERAL SAMPLING OF APOLOGETICS II

TWO ANALYTICAL PRESUPPOSITIONALISTS

Edward Carnell and Bernard Ramm have distinguished themselves as verificational apologists who attempt to develop the Christian defense from truth tests used in combination. The late Edward John Carnell was President and Professor of Philosophical Apologetics and Systematic Theology at Fuller Theological Seminary in Pasadena, California. The late Bernard L. Ramm was a professor of theology at a number of Baptist institutions throughout his career. Carnell was known for numerous books on apologetics, notably his *Introduction to Christian Apologetics*. Bernard Ramm also wrote several books dealing with apologetic issues, but his method is outlined in *The God Who Makes a Difference*.[1]

Edward Carnell

John Warwick Montgomery calls Carnell "the finest philosophical apologist of the 20th Century."[2] This assessment would be shared by a number of outstanding apologists who trace their own development to Carnell's writing and dynamic teaching style.[3] Carnell is really a transitional figure between evidentialism and classical apologetics and the presuppositionalism of Van Til. This is largely due to the formative influences of Gordon Clark and Cornelius Van Til on his thinking.[4]

---

[1] Bernard L. Ramm, *The God Who Makes a Difference: A Christian Appeal to Reason* (Waco: Word, Incorporated, 1972).

[2] Montgomery, A History of Apologetics, 45.

[3] See Gordon R. Lewis, "Edward John Carnell,' in *Handbook of Evangelical Theologians*, ed. Walter A. Elwell (Grand Rapids: Baker Book House, 1993), 321-337.

[4] Carnell, *Introduction to Christian Apologetics*, 9, 41n22.

Carnell's commitment to logic was nurtured by Clark, and his emphasis on the Trinity as the solution to the Problem of the One and the Many was inspired by Van Til. Carnell's critique of empiricism is clearly in line with that of both Clark and Van Til and represents his major point of departure from evidentialism and classical apologetics.[5] Carnell's rejection of empiricism is the basis of his critique of natural theology and the theistic proofs of Aquinas: "Thomas is closed up to all the problems of a *tabula rasa* epistemology."[6] Like Clark and Van Til before him, Carnell considered the modern philosophical critique of the proofs as the last word on their failure. Universal and necessary truth simply "cannot be derived from an analysis of sense perception, for from flux only flux can come." Therefore, Thomism's "fatal empirical epistemology" is unsuccessful.[7]

In the end, Carnell agrees with modern philosophers that Aquinas was out to merely Christianize Aristotle's God. The fact that Aristotle did not come to Christian conclusions in the end is evidence of the "fallacy of anticipation" in Aquinas' thinking. At best, Aquinas proves the existence of the god of Aristotle, not the Trinitarian God of the Bible. Throughout his discussion, Carnell affirms the cogency of Hume's arguments against the proofs.[8]

Carnell summarizes the legacy of empiricism in the following words: "The story of empiricism, from Heraclitus to Hume, is a short history of skepticism."[9] The problem is located in the fundamental principle of empiricism: There is nothing in the intellect that was not first in the senses. To overcome this problem, a transition to Christian rationalism is necessary. Valid truths are based on prior "innate criteria" given by the creator to guide our pursuit of the true, the beautiful, and the good (Augustine). Therefore, the Christian follows the *a priori* method, which begins with God and ends with the facts. Apart from this order, one ends

---

[5] Ibid., 34-37.

[6] Ibid., 126.

[7] Ibid., 139.

[8] Ibid., 129-139. The pervasive influence of Hume's critique of the proofs among evangelicals is evidenced by the scarcity of rebuttals in the apologetic literature. A good example that is worthy of consideration is offered by John Gerstner in *Classical Apologetics*, 93-136.

[9] Ibid., 152.

with neither God nor the facts.¹⁰ Apriorism, then, is the answer to the flux of empiricism. Truth, goodness, and beauty require universal and necessary criteria apprehended in the soul and perceived through the analysis of the content of reason itself.¹¹

In considering Carnell's antidote to empiricism, it is interesting to notice that he conceives of epistemology as having only two alternatives: Sensationalism or innate ideas. This is clearly evident in his explanation of the principle of empiricism stated above: "A presupposition followed by the empiricists, Aristotle, Aquinas, and Locke, but which was rejected by the rationalists, Plato, Augustine, and Leibniz. The mind is a *tabula rasa*."¹² Through reading Carnell, one would never come to the idea that there are empiricists who acknowledge an *a priori* aspect to knowledge; he seemed to believe that all empiricism is crass sensationalism and that an epistemology of innate ideas is the only alternative.¹³ And yet, even the "pure empiricism" of Buswell requires that the laws of reason are *a priori*, finding their ultimate source and explanation in God himself.¹⁴ Undoubt-

---

¹⁰ Ibid., 152-153. It is important to note that Carnell is following Clark, who is following Augustine. The last part of this citation is Carnell's quotation of Clark's book, *A Christian Philosophy of Education*, a source often quoted throughout Carnell's *Introduction*.

¹¹ Ibid. 153.

¹² Ibid., 367.

¹³ Once again, the distinction between ontological and epistemic presuppositions is at issue. Is the *epistemic* assumption of *a priori* truths really necessary as a starting point for knowledge (Carnell)? If the ontological necessity of *a priori* truths is *discovered* in the process of thinking (Buswell), is not the problem of empiricism solved? In the end, the necessity of *a priori* truths is established but in two different ways. This controversy is the epistemological root of the controversy in apologetics over presuppositions. The argument of Christian rationalism for innate ideas is the root of the argument for presupposing Christian theism as an epistemic starting point. What is of greatest importance here is the observation that the necessity of *a priori* truths is *not* in dispute among evangelical apologists. Arguments over rationalism and empiricism tend to obscure this and to further confusion and poor communication where clarity is most needed. The fundamental rift in epistemology and apologetics centers on the question of starting point.

¹⁴ It is interesting that Gordon Lewis, a very close follower of Carnell, chose the term "pure empiricism" to describe Buswell, despite the fact that

edly, categorical presuppositionalists would see this as a crucial oversight on Carnell's part, one that determines his evaluation of natural theology and theistic proofs.

Through the analysis of the content of rationality, it is possible to come to universal and necessary truth about the true, the good and the beautiful. What are the truths or eternal concepts that make up this body of innate ideas? The basic principles of logic, ethics and aesthetics are unique to mankind. These principles suggest the Christian God as their author, as Carnell points out in his discussion of logic. The soul knows God through knowing its divine endowments, recognizing the "transtemporal, trans-spatial Mind" that sustains "the timeless character of logic." Thus, we are made logical beings, and creation in the divine image offers a "workable hypothesis in light of the evidence."[15]

Carnell appends an important footnote to these comments on logic: "Let us remember that we are not attempting a *demonstration* of God's existence; we are simply pointing out the presence of data which make the hypothesis of God's existence coherent."[16] If not for this qualification, we might assume that Carnell's defense of eternal truths is at bottom no different than Buswell's. For if God is ultimately necessary to account for the laws of logic, then what difference does it make whether they are innate ideas or discovered in the process of experience? But Carnell does not want to argue for the necessity of God's existence since, as he says, "God gets in the way of all demonstration of deity." Proposing God as a "workable hypothesis" does not beg the question of God and provides an adequate basis for Christian commitment because the hypothesis is "coherent."

The character of analytical presuppositionalism over against that of categorical presuppositionalism is clearly revealed by this approach to the laws of logic. Categorical presuppositionalists recognize, as Carnell does, that "the brute bumping of undirected atoms" is not a sufficient condition for reliable laws of logic. But through the application of epistemological first principles, the existence of God becomes more than a coherent and workable hypothesis, even if the God of the proof does not rise to all the

---

Buswell's carefully qualified affirmation of *a priori* laws of reason is fundamental to his epistemology.

[15] Ibid., 164.

[16] Ibid.

specifications of the Christian faith. God does not get in the way of the demonstration because God is not an epistemological first principle. In short, God is not presupposed in the same way first principles are, which is why the proof does not beg the question.[17] God may be ultimately necessary to account for first principles, but the use of first principles may also be justified on the grounds of their undeniability and utility.

Carnell was not compelled by this way of thinking because he did not believe that the systematic application of eternal concepts to facts necessarily led to theism. Facts are subject to many interpretations at the personal and metaphysical levels; only at the scientific level do we find common ground in the interpretation of facts. While the line that separates scientific and metaphysical judgments is "almost invisible, we can assuredly assume that there is a point where science leaves off and metaphysics begins." There is, however, no neutrality in metaphysics, which means that the logical starting point of the Christian and non-Christian differ radically. At the level of ultimate meaning, then, "the system of Christianity and the system of non-Christianity have absolutely no truth in common." This makes an appropriate logical starting point an essential "clue" to true meaning.[18]

We notice that the Christian's logical starting point only provides a "clue" because it may not be taken for granted from the outset. In reality though, "one is inside a system of philosophy before he knows the details of just how he arrived there."[19] Carnell refers to Christian theism as an assumption, but it is also a *hypothetical* interpretation of facts that requires testing.[20] In order to test the Christian interpretation, another starting point is required. While the logical starting point is the "highest principle" of interpretive unity and order, the "synoptic starting point" proves the logical starting point by serving as a "primitive starting procedure" or method of verification.[21]

---

[17] First principles are epistemologically necessary, but God is ontologically necessary. Thus, the necessity of God's existence is demonstrated through the application of first principles to experience.

[18] Ibid., 215.

[19] Ibid., 122.

[20] Ibid., 91-92.

[21] Ibid., 124-125.

The "primitive starting procedure" referred to is that of systematic consistency: "It is *consistency* because it is based upon a rigid application of the law of contradiction, and it is a *systematic* consistency because the data which are formed into this consistent system are taken from the totality of our experience from within and without." This procedure combines facts with logic into a "double approach" that avoids both uninterpreted facts and a merely formal system of belief. Consistency provides a negative worldview test and being systematic provides an affirmative test.[22]

The outcome of this procedure in testing the Christian hypothesis is not demonstrative certainty; in fact, the proof for any worldview "cannot rise above rational probability."[23] For Carnell, this is really not a liability for a couple of reasons. First, it means that the case against Christianity is also only probable. Therefore, if the Christian's faith is grounded in better evidence than what is offered for competing worldviews, then there is no reason to fear claims of a demonstrative case against Christianity. The Christian system can be refuted only by probability, so "perhaps our loss is our gain."[24] Also, the Christian does not want to give undue emphasis to logic and reason, thereby neglecting the necessary roles of faith and the Holy Spirit in producing certainty:

> It is this union of faith and truth that makes it possible to construct a Christian apologetics. But apologetics can only prepare the heart for faith, for faith is a gift from God. Logic can be the means by which the Spirit leads a man into faith, but it is the Spirit, not logic, which finally seals the faith to the heart.[25]

Evangelical apologists recognize that the Bible speaks to the dynamics of Christian commitment and disallows a purely intellectual approach to matters of proof and certainty. For Carnell, probability combines with moral or subjective assurance to produce moral certainty. Moral assurance grasps the "strength of the evidence" for the Christian "meaning-pattern" as sufficient to compel faith. What the mind detects, then, is a "state of

---

[22] Ibid., 60-61.

[23] Ibid., 113.

[24] Ibid., 115n15.

[25] Ibid., 70.

coherence" that naturally leads to a "complete moral or subjective certainty." In this view, perfect rational certainty is not necessary, since the mind and heart are seeking coherent evidence, not perfect evidence.[26]

This is truly one of the best statements of the meaning of Christian assurance in the literature of apologetics. The "state of coherence" Carnell refers to is not merely the logical coherence of Christian theism as a worldview. Rather, he is talking about the coherence of the *evidence* for the Christian faith: "The evidences for the Way—their nature, extent, and interlocking—create in the Christian a powerful impulse in the direction of Christianity's truth."[27] This explanation has a kind of universality to it because it explains why different apologetic methods lead to Christian certitude. While evidences and arguments differ among apologists, all apologetic systems strive to present a coherent set of arguments and evidences for the Christian faith. Given faith, the witness of the Holy Spirit, and the coherence of Christian theism and its evidence, Christian truth will be accepted beyond a morally reasonable doubt.

Bernard Ramm

In terms of creative theological and apologetical output, few contemporary evangelicals have risen to the heights of Bernard Ramm.[28] Some of his offerings became standard evangelical textbooks for over a generation.[29-30] His later theological work especially is controversial, reflecting a critical appreciation for Karl Barth that accounts for much of the ecumenical emphasis of his work.[31-32] An early textbook on apologetics presented

---

[26] Ibid., 117-118.

[27] Ibid., 118.

[28] Kevin J. Vanhoozer, "Bernard Ramm," in *Handbook of Evangelical Theologians*, 290-306.

[29] Bernard L. Ramm, *Protestant Biblical Interpretation* (Grand Rapids: Baker Book House, 1970).

[30] Bernard L. Ramm, *The Christian View of Science and Scripture* (Grand Rapids: Wm. B. Eerdmans Publishing Co., 1954).

[31] Bernard L. Ramm, *After Fundamentalism: The Future of Evangelical Theology* (San Francisco: Harper and Row Publishers, 1983).

[32] Bernard L. Ramm, *Offense to Reason: The Theology of Sin* (San Francisco: Harper and Row Publishers, 1985).

standard arguments in defense of Christianity, placing special emphasis on the Bible's internal evidence for its inspiration and supernatural character.[33] Over time, Ramm assembled the pieces of a comprehensive apologetic, which he summarizes in *The God Who Makes a Difference*.

Ramm's creativity was expressed in an attempt to synthesize the apologetic insights of the Reformation, specifically those of John Calvin and Abraham Kuyper. Of course, neither Calvin nor Kuyper placed a major emphasis on apologetics understood in its more traditional sense. But in their development of the doctrine of the witness of the Holy Spirit, Ramm saw the key to a biblical apologetic. Through further inspiration from Carnell and Clark, he saw a way to bring the most important contributions of Reformed thinking on apologetics into a systematic framework.[34]

Ramm was especially concerned to show that there is a coherent theory of apologetics underlying Calvin's limited apologetical statements. Chapter eight of the *Institutes* is believed by some to be inconsistent with Calvin's remarks in chapter seven. Ramm agrees with others who argue that Calvin was aware of the possible charge of subjectivism in light of his emphasis on the witness of the Holy Spirit. By stressing the evidential materials in the Scriptures themselves, Calvin avoids this charge without compromising the heart of apologetics.[35] In simplest terms, Ramm's own apologetic is little more than an elaboration of Calvin's approach. Among evangelical apologists, it is doubtful that anyone represents Calvin's concerns as faithfully as Ramm.[36]

---

[33] Bernard L. Ramm, *Protestant Christian Evidences: A Textbook of the Evidences of the Truthfulness of the Christian Faith for Conservative Protestants* (Chicago: Mood Press, 1953).

[34] Ramm, *The God Who Makes a Difference*, 11.

[35] Ibid., 56-57.

[36] Followers of Van Til consider themselves the true heirs of Calvin in the area of apologetics. This is questionable, however, in light of the philosophically uncomplicated structure of Calvin's apologetic. Van Til expresses Calvin's concerns according to a Christian version of an idealist epistemology. As an Augustinian, Calvin viewed facts from a moral and spiritual point of view. Van Til, on the other hand, adds an epistemological dimension to factuality that is totally lacking in Calvin. Ramm attempts to provide a synthesis of Calvin's views based on the original Augustinian context of his thinking. As a result, Ramm's modern perspective brings

What kind of apologetic is able to bring the witness of the Holy Spirit and the witness of evidences together? Ramm believed that a verificational approach serves this purpose best. He acknowledges the roots of his own approach in Brightman and Carnell, who advocated "the theory that truth is a combination of logical consistency and conformity to fact."[37] Like Carnell, Ramm is critical of the theistic proofs.[38] He is also not concerned to discuss the role of epistemological first principles, presumably because they are the building blocks of the theistic proofs. Ramm also does not deal with the epistemological controversy over the derivation of concepts. Truth is verified as a pattern of belief, which means that a worldview and its corresponding epistemology must be verified as a whole. We don't decide beforehand how concepts are derived and then build a worldview with them. In the end, the worldview that combines logical consistency and factual adequacy provides a theory of concepts:

> Individual facts, no matter how many of them, do not constitute effective knowledge. Facts must be interpreted, and the interpretation is stated in the form of a theory, a hypothesis, a generalization, or a law. This is true whether one is considering physics or philosophy.[39]

Thus, the interpretive power of the Christian worldview is both the basis of its appeal and its verification.[40] A verificational apologetic necessarily begins with the hypothesis of both the general and specific definitions of the Christian faith, making it a Trinitarian apologetic.[41] It therefore pre-

---

more clarification to Calvin, whereas Van Til really translates Calvin's insights according to a post-Kantian paradigm.

[37] Ibid., 75.

[38] Ramm states the arguments against the proofs but does not openly agree with these arguments. He simply states the traditional criticisms without personal comment. His own problem with them has more to do with their lack of utility than with their lack of cogency, although he implicitly seems to agree with the modern critique. Like other critics of the proofs, Ramm feels that they simply do not verify Christian theism, which is the goal of apologetics.

[39] Ibid., 32.

[40] Ibid., 18.

[41] Ibid., 36.

supposes the priority of revelation over human philosophy, the effects of sin on the will and passions, and the necessity of faith and illumination to its reception.[42] Like Augustine, Ramm says that belief is necessary to understanding. Augustine recognized that love is the basis of learning. A student who hates the teacher learns little, but the student who loves the teacher learns readily. Similarly, God is known as God is loved, but God is loved only in redemption. Therefore, faith brings redemption, redemption brings love, and love brings full understanding. Some understanding, however, must come first in this order. The experience of faith cannot be purely mystical and separate from the Bible, theology, and the valid insights of psychology.[43]

This Augustinian view of knowledge implies a definite approach to Christian evidences that conflicts with other approaches. *Evidentialists* attempt to establish the Christian faith by a two-step process, using "historical faith as a bridge from unbelief to saving faith."[44] This approach falls short, however, because the effect of sin on human reason and the complexity of verifying theological beliefs and divine revelations are not sufficiently taken into account.

Probabilists have the same problems, despite more modest claims. Even if a more favorable attitude toward the Christian faith can be encouraged by Christian evidences, "can historical faith really buck successfully the sinful disposition of man? As a matter of fact, only a very small percentage of Christian converts go through the process of moving from historical faith to saving faith."[45]

---

[42] In line with Carnell, Ramm presupposes Christian theism, but not in the same way as the metaphysical presuppositionalists. As a hypothetical assumption, the theory must be tested; it is not accepted from the start as necessary to the possibility of predication. Predication is possible on the basis of common ground.

[43] Ibid., 37.

[44] Ibid., 55.

[45] Ibid., 55-56. This point is certainly arguable. While most converts would not describe their conversion as a two-step process through historical faith to saving faith, the two steps may nevertheless be distinguishable upon more careful analysis. Most people believe in the existence of God prior to becoming Christians. It is a rare person who moves from atheism directly to Christian theism. In fact, Geisler might argue that historical faith is engendered by a normal process of cosmological reasoning that

Negativists dispense with Christian evidences altogether due to a preoccupation with philosophical apologetics. They might also neglect evidences because "a man will believe in evidences only if on philosophical grounds he believes Christianity to be true." From this perspective, evidences become part of the biblical witness, but they have no apologetic value or function.[46]

Ramm's view of Christian evidences has been sketched above as an elaboration of Calvin's approach. It remains to detail his method of verification, which he calls "the three concentric circles" of verification.[47] This method provides a proper context in which to understand the use and function of evidences and to avoid the problems of other inadequate approaches. With his approach, Ramm has attempted to marry the basic structure of Carnell's apologetic with the priorities of Scripture and the biblical insights of Augustine and Calvin. The creativity and wisdom expressed in the accomplishment of this task establishes him as one of the truly great evangelical apologists of recent times.

The first concentric circle of verification is the persuasion and witness of the Holy Spirit. While this inner circle of verification involves subjectivity, it does not reduce to subjectivism. Ramm is concerned to emphasize the objective character of this testimony as a witness. The problem with

---

leads most people to belief in God long before they encounter a Christian evangelist or apologist. In effect, God is the apologist of historical faith through His revelation in creation (ROM 1:20). The Christian apologist may take over from here, making the case specifically for Christian theism. But the fact that verificational apologists successfully defend Christian theism as a whole does not prove that historical faith plays no part in most conversions. The operative assumption of verificationalists is that any faith that falls short of saving faith is inadequate since it does not *necessarily* provide a bridge to saving faith. Evidentialists and classical apologists, on the other hand, assume that historical faith is valuable, even if it is not an infallible bridge to saving faith in every case.

[46] Ibid., 56. While Ramm does not mention Van Til by name, it is difficult not to see a veiled reference to Van Til in Ramm's description of a negative attitude toward Christian evidences. While Van Til denied dispensing with evidences, he also made it clear that evidences do not function apart from the acceptance of Christian theism as a necessary context for their intelligibility. From Ramm's perspective, this constitutes a negative view of evidences.

[47] Ibid., 38.

Christian evidences is that they are accepted as evidences only after illumination by faith and by virtue of the witness of the Spirit. In ancient Greek courts, a witness testified to personally observed facts and persuaded the court that the facts were true. This two-fold idea of testimony and persuasion describes the "juridical or forensic character" of the Spirit's witness. Thus the Holy Spirit is required to verify the testimony of Scripture and its evidences and to persuade the hearer of their truth.[48]

One reason the Spirit's witness does not reduce to subjectivism is that the Christian faith is *autopistic*—believable in itself: "Christianity is credible, believable, within itself and therefore need not depend on externals for verification."[49] Provided the Spirit's witness is always understood in connection with the Word of God, it remains firmly anchored. The Holy Spirit first bears witness to Jesus Christ and the gospel. This is presented by John as a unified witness: "For there are three that testify: the Spirit, the water and the blood; and the three are in agreement" (1Jo 5:7-8). The water and blood describe Christ's life from his baptism (water) to his death (blood), thus showing that "the gospel facts represent the external fulcrum of the witness of the Spirit."[50]

The result of this witness is nothing less than full persuasion, a fullness of conviction all believers have, even if they are not conscious of the witnessing of the Holy Spirit. The knowledge of theology, apologetics, or philosophy is not required in order to experience the certainty of the Spirit's persuasion. There is, however, an additional aspect to the Spirit's witness that is required for saving faith, which is taken from the intellectual world of learning. This model describes the witness of the Spirit as illumination.[51]

Illumination is another of the "concepts of power" associated with salvation. The importance of such concepts in apologetics is to "forbid any interpretation that makes faith a dry, powerless act of the intellect."[52] The burden of Ramm's entire approach is to avoid an arid intellectualism in

---

[48] Ibid., 39-40.

[49] Ibid., 41.

[50] Ibid.

[51] Ibid., 42.

[52] Ibid,. 43.

apologetics and to preserve its spiritual center. Without this inner circle of verification, "the case is deeded away to a method of verification alien to religion. In other terms, only God can speak for God."[53]

The second concentric circle of verification encompasses the action of God in creation and history. The witness of the Spirit is adequate by itself, and most believers experience the certainty of faith on the basis of this witness alone. Nor is faith based on the Spirit's witness mere subjectivism; it would be better described as subjectivity because it is directed to the inner life. But the Christian gospel is more than faith as subjectivity because there are objective elements in Scripture that witness to the divine origin and truthfulness of the biblical revelation.[54]

In less literate times, there was neither the time nor learning to develop a comprehensive apologetic. Therefore, the witness of the Spirit served the redemptive purpose of God through supernatural and spiritual means. Indeed, there are still many situations were a well-reasoned defense of the faith is not offered along with the gospel due to a lack of literacy on the part of either the preacher or the listeners. Nevertheless, evidences are a part of the Christian witness, being woven into the very fabric of the scriptural witness itself. As part of the Bible's witness to itself, these divine revelations and actions become foundations of the Christian's experience and justify its authenticity. The internal experiences of salvation are based on external historical realities. In this way, "the truth of God and the action of God are both the presupposition and the test of Christian experiences."[55]

In line with Calvin, Ramm points to the scriptural *indicia* as the content of this second circle of Christian witness. Miracles and prophecy formed the substance of the apologetic of the early Church, and they will serve the needs of the Church today, even though they require a more strident philosophical defense because of modern attacks. Miracles especially demonstrate that "God is here at work in our space, in our time, and in our order of nature.... Theology that rejects the supernatural and miraculous is only word, promise, speculation, or philosophy."[56] Christi-

---

[53] Ibid., 44.

[54] Ibid., 47.

[55] Ibid., 51.

[56] Ibid., 54.

anity excels all other belief systems in that "the internal witness of the Spirit is paralleled by the external actions of God in Event and Word."[57]

The third concentric circle of verification is that of synoptic vision, by which Ramm means a meaningful and integrated pattern of belief:

> In order to acquire a synoptic vision, the scholar looks over the whole field of his specialty. He tries to see it as a totality, a system, an organism, and not just a heap of facts. The term *vision* indicates a pattern, a configuration, a model, a picture, a complex diagrammatic interpretation. That pattern or that picture which has the most appeal to him, that puts things together for him in the most meaningful way even with the lack of a great number of important data, is the one he chooses. That is his synoptic vision.[58]

Ramm uses a number of descriptive phrases to explain this aspect of verification. A synoptic vision is a "synthesized world," it is similar to what existentialists call *decision*, it is "honest with the facts," and it includes many elements, facts, and interpretations.[59] A responsible synoptic vision must also have a measure of coherence. Coherence must be understood in light of biblical mysteries; it is not therefore to be taken in terms of a complete or perfect coherence. Perfect consistency is not possible due to certain problems or difficulties we encounter in the Bible. Doctrines like the incarnation and the relationship of God's sovereignty to human freedom must be understood according to the "principle of complementarity." The test of coherence is not applicable in these contexts, but nor is it violated by the above principle. There are also biblical difficulties that do not readily submit to the test of coherence. While coherent solutions to most biblical problems have been proposed, some problems remain. In fact, "such kinds of problems beset any system." Nevertheless, "there is enough consistency in the scriptural record itself and in the main Christian doctrines to warrant responsible belief."[60]

---

[57] Ibid., 52.

[58] Ibid., 60. Note the similarity here to Carnell's synoptic starting point.

[59] Ibid., 60, 61, 63-64.

[60] Ibid., 68-69.

The result of a comprehensive approach to verification is that the Christian becomes convinced of the truth of his faith:

> He is convinced of the truth of his faith by the witness of the Spirit. He is convinced of the truth of his faith by the actions of the living God in the cosmos which makes a difference. And he is a Christian because he believes that the Christian faith gives him the most adequate synoptic vision there is with reference to man, humanity, the world, and God.[61]

But what does it mean to be convinced? According to Ramm, the Christian faith is held with *certitude* rather than *certainty*: "Certitude expresses a degree of psychological or spiritual persuasion. Certainty expresses the state of the evidence for a particular belief."[62] This distinction is important in apologetics, and it is not always made with Ramm's care and precision. Strictly speaking, it is inaccurate to say that the case for Christianity is merely probable. In fact, the case is spiritually certain and factually probable according to Ramm's apologetic. The witness of the Spirit to the saving revelation of Christ and the gospel warrants a "full spiritual certitude" that does not apply to the "historical side" of Christianity given the probable nature of all historical judgments. Therefore, the "logical status" of Christianity is highly probable, but the convictional status is fully certain.[63] For Ramm, this disproportion between faith and the logical status of Christian evidences justifies the indispensable role of the witness of the Holy Spirit in salvation and in apologetics.

---

[61] Ibid., 61.

[62] Ibid., 73.

[63] Ibid.

Chapter 4

A GENERAL SAMPLING OF APOLOGETICS III

Two Metaphysical Presuppositionalists

Cornelius Van Til and John Frame are referred to as presuppositional apologists because of their commitment to Christian theism as the necessary starting point for knowledge.[1] The late Cornelius Van Til was Professor of Apologetics at Westminster Theological Seminary in Philadelphia, Pennsylvania. John M. Frame formerly held the J.D. Trimble Chair of Systematic Theology and Philosophy at Reformed Theological Seminary in Orlando, Florida. Van Til is arguably the most controversial apologist of the 20th Century. The radically different structure of his apologetic drew either praise or criticism from almost every segment of conservative Protestantism. Frame, on the other hand, has developed presuppositional apologetics along more ecumenical lines, attempting to bridge some of the gaps between evangelicals and presuppositionalists that resulted from the strong polemics of Van Til.

Cornelius Van Til

The Defense of the Faith, by Cornelius Van Til, is the foundational text in presuppositional apologetics. While this view represents the minority approach to apologetics among evangelical Christians, it has nevertheless had tremendous influence since its introduction by Van Til in the 1930's.[2] Perhaps even more important is the fact that Van Til has taught many of the prominent evangelical apologists of recent times. Edward Carnell,

---

[1] Since all evangelical apologists are presuppositional in some sense according to the analytical framework of this study, it is somewhat confusing to refer to the Van Til school as *the* presuppositional school of apologetics. It should become evident that the radically different manner in which presuppositions are held by this school justifies the label.

[2] See John M. Frame, "Cornelius Van Til," in *Handbook of Evangelical Theologians*, 156-167.

Francis Schaeffer, Greg Bahnsen, and John Frame are four of Van Til's more famous students. While Bahnsen and Frame have remained fairly close to Van Til's own position, Frame has ventured to offer corrections and improvements to the presuppositional system. Both Carnell and Schaeffer moved farther away from Van Til, but his influence is still evident in their apologetic writings. The tremendous influence of presuppositionalism in apologetical circles may be attributed to Van Til's longevity at Westminster (over 40 years of teaching), an extensive bibliography of written work, and a solid corps of excellent students who went on to distinguish themselves in the field of apologetics.

Van Til was no stranger to controversy. He engaged everyone who opposed his apologetic, from fellow evangelicals to liberal and neo-orthodox scholars. He had a "take no prisoners" attitude when it came to confronting his critics, which made him even more provocative and influential in the long run. Van Til was not one to seek a position of compromise when it came to ideas. This attitude has everything to do with his theory of knowledge and apologetics, as an explanation of his apologetic will show.

For many evangelicals, understanding Van Til is not easy. The evidentialist mentality, which characterizes much of evangelical apologetics, is simply so foreign to this apologist's way of thinking that many readers have trouble getting on his wavelength. While his writing style is actually quite straightforward and illustrative, he uses generally unfamiliar terminology from German Idealism, giving it his own particular spin. Van Til was also a specialist in metaphysics, especially that of Hegel. He did his Ph.D. dissertation at Princeton University on the idealism of Hegel, Bradley, and Bosanquet. The popularity of idealism during the early part of the last century had a formative influence on him, along with the Christian influences of Abraham Kuyper and Herman Bavinck.

The difficulty of Van Til's terminology is something his critics often brought up. His own response was that he was merely following the example of the Apostles, who also reinterpreted the philosophical language of their day according to their biblical worldview.[3] Certainly Van Til is justified on this point. It is interesting, however, that he chose the language of idealism as his vehicle for a biblical apologetic. Most Christian philosophers would not choose this language, which raises the question of why Van Til preferred it. Though he was careful to reject the *teachings* of

---

[3] Van Til, *Defense of the Faith*, 40n1.

idealism as unbiblical, there must be some formal similarity between idealism and his own view of Christian philosophy, or else why would he choose this terminology? John's use of the term *logos* is also based on a formal similarity between Christianity and Greek philosophy concerning the Logos. Therefore, Van Til's critics were at least partially justified in having suspicions about his language.

For all its seeming verbal complexity, the apologetic of Van Til is remarkably simple. This simplicity is, no doubt, one reason for its appeal. For the reader who prefers a simple statement of Van Til's position, the essay, "My Credo," in E. R. Geehan's *Jerusalem and Athens*, is the best summary available.[4] Van Til's first point in that essay summarizes the entire apologetic: "The self-attesting Christ of Scripture has always been my starting point for everything I have said."[5] This general statement explains the unusual arrangement of *The Defense of the Faith*. Unlike most books on apologetics, this one begins with a summation of the specific expression of faith that its author intends to defend.

For Van Til, the *what* always precedes the *that*. In other words, what exists determines how we know it. This is why *The Defense of the Faith* begins with a statement of Christian theology. The theology elaborated here is that of the Reformed faith. Apart from Calvinism, the Christian faith cannot be adequately defended. For it is the sovereignty of God that guarantees God's ability to interpret the universe and even his ability to interpret himself over against the universe. Equally important is the doctrine of the Trinity. According to a Christian view of reality, the Trinity alone enables an answer to the fundamental metaphysical Problem of the One and the Many.

The Godhead is the source for unified diversity in the world since God is a unified diversity within Himself: "In God's being there are no particulars not related to the universal and there is nothing universal that is not fully expressed in the particulars."[6] Thus, God is the "concrete universal" of Christianity. God as the concrete universal answers the One-and-Many problem by providing a basis to bring the many into contact with one another. Without a concrete universal, all particulars would "abstract

---

[4] Van Til, "My Credo," in *Jerusalem and Athens*, 1-21.

[5] Ibid., 3.

[6] Van Til, *Defense of the Faith*, 43.

particulars"—unordered and therefore meaningless. However, unity among particulars comes through generalizing, "by abstracting from particulars in order to include them into larger unities." This effectively strips the particulars of their individuality, leading to an abstract universal that is out of contact with the particulars. Therefore, the universal—in order to be truly concrete—must be adequate to unify the particulars without destroying their particularity.[7] Does the Christian God meet this requirement?

By virtue of his own triune nature, God has complete self-knowledge, and by virtue of creation, temporal diversity is comprehensively interpreted according to the plan of God. Because the concrete universal is personal, the particulars of both the Creator and the creature remain in a perfect unity.

Given the problem of knowledge as Van Til conceives of it, it is not difficult to understand why he rejects all other apologetic systems that begin "from below." Starting from himself, mankind is set adrift on the shoreless sea of disjointed facts, unable to interpret himself or the things around him. God would also be in the same boat with humanity if not for his aseity and absolute sovereign control over all things. The failure of idealism is that it attempts to assume the position of God above all the facts, forgetting that the idealist philosopher is himself just another abstract particular. This problem is complicated further by the fall of mankind and his faculties. Not only are human beings epistemologically lost without God, but they are also ethically lost due to their antagonism toward the truth. In short, mankind is lost and wants to stay that way. Through the curse, fallen man ignores his need for a concrete universal outside of himself and proudly confers upon himself the prerogative of being his own universal, his own autonomous interpreter.

This explains why Van Til rejects the notion of brute factuality. Facts are not self-interpreting because they require universals to bring them into relationship with one another. Since an abstract universal is not sufficient to the task, God is required to interpret facts and their relationships for us. Again, an immanentistic perspective wrongly assumes that facts bespeak their own interpretation, contrary to the approach to the Problem of the One and the Many explained above.

---

[7] Ibid., 42-43.

It is on this basis that Van Til argues that we must begin with the self-attesting Christ of Scripture as the only guarantee of knowledge. What Van Til means by self-attesting is confusing to some who think of this term in a fideistic sense. What he means is that the presupposition of the Christ of Scripture is required to make sense of anything at all. In other words, the transcendental necessity of Christ to knowing anything at all is the proof that Christ is the Son of God, the Second Person of the Trinity, and who he says he is. He is self-attesting because he is transcendentally necessary.

Van Til's notion of the point of contact is also a logical extension of the self-attesting Christ of Scripture. The point of contact with the non-Christian cannot be found in the realm of common notions. If Christ is necessary to interpret any and all facts, then how could the non-Christian's interpretation of the facts be the same as the Christian's, since the non-Christian does not believe in Christ? He has already interpreted himself and the world according to his sinful, autonomous perspective. He begins "from below," but the Christian begins "from above." There must be, then, another point from which the believer can appeal to the non-Christian.

This point of contact is to be found in the universal sense of deity. According to Romans 1, all men know God, even if they are suppressing that truth in unrighteousness. By virtue of suppression, the non-Christian holds down the truth, but it is not destroyed. So while consciously the non-Christian denies any knowledge of God, subconsciously he knows the true God exists and has claims on his life. Van Til faults the Roman Catholic and Arminian views for ascribing self-sufficiency to the human mind. In light of this error, they consistently fail to challenge the non-Christian's pretended autonomy. Reformed theologians, however, view the human mind as derivative and in constant contact with divine revelation (ROM 1:20).[8]

It is clear that Van Til does not deny common ground per se, as some apologists claim that he does. He affirms a common world but not a common worldview. Since all men live within the environment of revelation, the problem of apologetics is not primarily epistemological; it is ethical. The non-Christian knows God but will not acknowledge it. Most apologists would not go as far as Van Til does in denying any common notions. Why does he rule out all common notions? Is it not legitimate to say that the

---

[8] Ibid., 107.

non-Christian understands as the Christian does to a point but does not see his facts in their larger metaphysical context? Here is Van Til's answer:

> Weighing and measuring and formal reasoning are but aspects of one unified act of interpretation. It is either the would be autonomous man, who weighs and measures what he thinks of as brute or bare facts by the help of what he thinks of as abstract impersonal principles, or it is the believer, knowing himself to be a creature of God, who weighs and measures what he thinks of as God-created facts by what he thinks of as God-created laws.[9]

If all interpretation is "one unified act," then of course it is not possible to speak of common notions at all, even if we are referring to the common belief that two plus two equals four.[10] It is this point especially that separates Van Til from virtually all other apologists. Most apologists do not believe that all interpretation is one unified act encompassing the empirical and the metaphysical. The reason for this obvious. When a believer speaks to an non-Christian about basic arithmetic, there is seldom any argument over the *truth* that two plus two equals four. If the Christian and non-Christian agree on this point, then it is logical to say that they hold at least some of the truth in common. If they shift their perspective in the metaphysical direction and begin to discuss why this simple equation is true, then a difference between them will certainly emerge. In fact, having a point of agreement between the Christian and non-Christian raises the possibility of discussing what kind of worldview accounts for the facts that both believer and unbeliever have in common.

How then do we account for Van Til's contention? Van Til simply extends the biblical antithesis between believer and unbeliever to a consistent outworking in apologetics. Other apologists press the antithesis as well, but they do not rule out the possibility of common notions in the process. While Van Til's point about the sense of deity as a point of contact is correct and would not be denied by apologists, it is not the only point of contact. After all, why must the issue be brought to an either/or decision when our experience confirms that there are legitimate areas of agreement between believers and unbelievers? In the end, most will simply not be

---

[9] Van Til, *The Works of Cornelius Van Til*, CD-ROM, Logos Research Systems, 1997.

[10] Van Til interacts with Dooyeweerd in his booklet, *Common Grace*, using exactly this example.

A General Sampling of Apologetics III

convinced that the antithesis of Scripture is being sacrificed by a carefully qualified understanding of common ground.

It remains only to sketch the method of defense in light of the self-attesting Christ of Scripture. Van Til explains this as reasoning by presupposition. This method is "indirect rather than direct." This means that issues of truth cannot be resolved by a direct appeal to facts but must press beyond to what makes facts intelligible in the first place. This is where one's worldview comes into play. The Christian and non-Christian must approach this problem indirectly by assuming each other's position for the sake of argument. Through this method, the Christian can show the non-Christian that facts are not facts—nor are they intelligible—on unbelieving presuppositions. What this procedure reveals is that all reasoning is undeniably circular and that one's starting-point, method, and conclusion are inescapably interdependent.[11]

Reasoning by presupposition is just another name for a transcendental argument. Some philosophers and apologists have branded this approach fideistic. While there are legitimate criticisms to offer in response to this approach, the charge of fideism is not accurate. An argument for the preconditions of a particular belief is truly a rational argument. Robert Knudsen refers to this approach as an argument from the impossibility of the contrary:

> Van Til has asserted again and again ... that one cannot prove Christianity directly. That is an impossible undertaking, because it is impossible to assume a stance outside of Christianity in a meaningful way from which such a proof could proceed. Thus, as we have said, Van Til must entrench himself within the walls of the Christian faith, and he must argue from the impossibility of the contrary. This method seeks to establish an indirect proof of the faith.[12]

It is important to recognize that though reasoning by presupposition involves an indirect proof, it is a proof nevertheless. The main problem with Van Til is not that he reasons by presupposition. Presuppositional or transcendental forms of argument are quite common and useful in apologetics. The point has been made that Van Til does not have a corner on

---

[11] Van Til, *The Defense of the Faith*, 116-118.

[12] Robert D. Knudsen, "Progressive and Regressive Tendencies in Christian Apologetics," in *Jerusalem and Athens*, 291.

this argument type; other apologists use it in various ways that are similar and different from Van Til's use. Francis Schaeffer, for example, devotes the third book of his apologetic trilogy to a transcendental argument for the Christian faith, but his context is more empirical. Robert Knudsen gives an excellent definition of this type of argument that will serve as a basis for a legitimate criticism of Van Til: "A transcendental argument moves from what is to the conditions underlying its possibility."[13]

The problem with Van Til's argument is that, even though he claims that the apologist must start "from above," a transcendental argument requires that one also start "from below." We must argue from "what is" to the conditions underlying its possibility. This means that we must know something of what is before we can determine its preconditions. But this is precisely what Van Til does not allow. We have seen that Van Til does not allow any valid knowledge of ourselves or the world apart from the self-attesting Christ of Scripture. If this is the case, then how can we discover the preconditions of mute facts? If there is no brute factuality, then the preconditions of our facts cannot be discovered from the facts themselves. Again, if we move from "what is" to the conditions underlying its possibility, then our facts must say something on their own or we simply cannot make the move.[14]

---

[13] Robert D. Knudsen, "The Transcendental Perspective of Westminster's Apologetic," *Westminster Theological Journal* 48 (1986): 228.

[14] Most apologists distinguish between a surface knowledge of facts and a metaphysical knowledge of facts. It should be clear from this criticism of Van Til that this distinction is not merely useful or allowable; it is absolutely necessary to employing a transcendental argument in the first place. If there is no valid knowledge of the order and meaning of the world that we may gain from observation alone, then how can we proceed to determine the preconditions for that order and meaning? Van Til does admit common grace, and he allows that the non-Christian's knowledge is true "as far as it goes." The basic principles of his apologetic however, do not seem to make allowances for genuine knowledge outside the Christian system. It seems clear, then, that he takes away by his principles what he seems to give by common grace. It is this problem that forces Van Til into an unacceptable circularity in his use of the transcendental argument: Only the Christian faith provides a meaningful basis for factuality, so the facts necessarily prove the truth of Christianity. If the facts and our basic epistemological equipment do not convey enough meaning to enable us to determine their preconditions, then any appeal to them in support of a worldview is viciously circular. *One cannot know that God is required to*

A General Sampling of Apologetics III 75

The presuppositional response to this criticism would be that the unintelligibility of brute facts does not derail the transcendental argument because Christian theism is necessary for a meaningful world *no matter what the facts are*. Facts don't reveal their preconditions; reason does.[15] Given Christian presuppositions, the facts are whatever God says they are, which is Van Til's point. The implication of this, however, is an obvious formalism that leaves no place for Christian evidences in the traditional sense.[16] Since God's interpretation of facts makes them what they are, they cannot witness to the truth independently. Therefore, the presuppositionalist's appeal to facts as evidence for the Christian faith is also circular, which is why his claim to using evidences rings hollow in the ears of critics who understand what he is really saying.[17] Such circularity was acceptable

---

account for the orderliness of the world unless one has some prior knowledge of the world as orderly. Had Van Til said that the Christian God is ontologically necessary rather than epistemologically necessary to knowledge, he would never have provoked the charge of circularity. But his unified view of interpretation does not allow the distinction between the ontological and the epistemic that has been stressed often throughout the study.

[15] The presuppositionalist's truth test could be labeled as *transcendental adequacy*, which is really just a form of coherentism. It is often not recognized as such because transcendental arguments do not have a typical deductive form. In fact, this truth test is a pure coherentism because of its total rejection of empiricism. For Van Til, the real is the rational; word and fact are separate in creation but not in interpretation.

[16] See the appendix on Thom Notaro's *Van Til & the Use of Evidence*.

[17] It is crucial to understand that the circularity of the transcendental argument proposed by Van Til is the key to the absolute certainty of faith within his system. Since logic is no more autonomous than facts, the soundness of a circular argument is derived from the authority of God, not from neutral standards by which we judge logical form. In essence, the circularity of this argument becomes the basis for the certainty of faith because all arguments are, in the nature of the case, circular. Logical certainty is the result because the conclusion follows necessarily from the premises within a circular argument. As long as the form is accepted as sound on God's authority, the proof is absolute! It is at this point, however, that the charge of fideism arises. One must accept God's authority first in order to accept the logic that proves his existence; therefore, to argue for God on the basis of an approach to logic that presupposes him is really at bottom just an act of will. Van Til could respond to this by saying that

to Van Til, but the critics have found it to be the stumbling block of his apologetic.

John Frame

Apologetics To the Glory of God, by John M. Frame, represents one of the significant offerings in apologetics in recent years. The importance of the book is three-fold: (1) It represents presuppositional apologetics, the minority position in apologetical circles; (2) It is written in a popular style, unlike the major works of Van Til, the father of the movement; (3) It is written by an innovator within the presuppositional camp. This third point is especially important in light of the fact that Frame was chosen as Van Til's successor at Westminster Seminary and has demonstrated in his other books his exceptional qualities as a scholar, apologist, and philosopher. Along with the late Greg L. Bahnsen, no one is better qualified to speak for presuppositionalism.[18] While Frame has written a more detailed work on Van Til, *Apologetics To the Glory of God* provides a clearer picture of the apologetical enterprise as he conceives it.[19]

---

the circularity of our basic commitment is accepted on the same basis that the Thomist accepts his epistemological first principles: Circularity is logically undeniable. If Van Til were to respond this way, he would be back in the camp of traditional apologetics because undeniability, not God alone, is the reason for his categorical acceptance of formal circularity. This is essentially Arthur Lindsley's point in *Classical Apologetics* (304-309). If Van Til grounds his system in God alone, he is a fideist, but if he gives other reasons for his system, then he is a traditionalist. This is the presuppositionalist's dilemma. Also, *a metaphysical presuppositionalist who resorts to undeniability to justify his first principle cannot begrudge this criterion to the categorical presuppositionalist who uses it to justify his first principles*. In my judgment, simply admitting the undeniability principle would make Van Til's transcendental coherentism more cogent.

[18] See Greg L. Bahnsen, *Van Til's Apologetic: Readings & Analysis* (Phillipsburg: Presbyterian and Reformed Publishing Company, 1998). This book will certainly become a standard, if not the standard, work on Van Til. Bahnsen has very few criticisms of Van Til, unlike Frame. Bahnsen interacts with Frame on many points in this comprehensive treatment of Van Til. Based on my own familiarity with these two giants of presuppositionalism, it is clear that Bahnsen is the purist and Frame is the progressive.

[19] See Frame, *Cornelius Van Til*. This book provides an excellent complement to Frame's popular book on apologetics. Students of presupposi-

After defining apologetics as giving a reason for the Christian hope, Frame begins his discussion of apologetics by dealing with the Lordship of Christ over apologetics. As one committed to 1 Peter 3:15, Frame believes that apologists are duty bound by their allegiance to Christ to set him apart as Lord in apologetics. This means that there can be no neutral reasoning with the non-Christian. Christ and his word are, therefore, the ultimate standard and criterion of truth, the fundamental presupposition of the Christian.

At this point, it might seem that Frame is advocating the same kind of circularity that Van Til has been charged with. In responding to the charge, Frame denies simple circularity, pointing out that our ultimate presupposition is not without empirical evidence.[20] If a Humean skeptic began to question the validity of our use of empirical evidence, Frame says that the Christian worldview validates our use of the evidence, just as the rationalist's worldview validates his use of reason. In this sense, the circularity of the Christian view is really no different than the circularity of any other philosophical position. What's more, the perspectival nature of the Christian argument allows the Christian to shift to other types of evidence more in line with the objector's personal epistemology if that becomes necessary. Since everything in creation reveals God, the Christian can turn to any type of evidence in order to justify his ultimate presupposition.[21] Communication with non-Christians is not stifled due to conflicting presuppositions; rather, all facts are a useful resource to appeal to the non-Christian. And since the non-Christian knows God (ROM 1:21), the Christian argument must ring true at some level.

---

tionalism could do no better than to compare Frame's comprehensive book on Van Til with Bahnsen's. In doing so, it becomes clear that Frame is making major alterations to Van Til, whereas Bahnsen is really just cleaning up terminology.

[20] Frame, *Apologetics to the Glory of God*, 11-12.

[21] Ibid., 12n16. For Frame, a presupposition is first in *eminence*, not temporally first. In other words, our presupposition is not arbitrarily chosen without reasons. Consistent with Van Til, Frame believes that one's presupposition of Christ and the Scriptures is demanded to make predication possible. This is at the heart of his transcendental argument. Presuppositions are not hypothetical (Carnell, Schaeffer); they are categorical and grounded in God's revelation of himself. On this basis, Frame would deny with Van Til any charge of fideism.

While Frame argues conclusively against the simple circularity of the Christian presupposition, there is, nevertheless, a seeming ambiguity at the heart of all this. On the one hand, the Christian presupposition is not arbitrarily chosen; it is chosen for reasons. The especially important reason to choose the Christian position is that it alone makes predication possible. How do we know this? Frame would say with Van Til that neither chance nor impersonal laws provide a basis to relate any two facts; only the presupposition of the triune God can solve the Problem of the One and the Many. On the other hand, Frame wants to encourage a direct appeal to the facts as evidence for the Christian's ultimate presupposition. A direct appeal to facts, however, is still really an indirect appeal to facts, since our ultimate presupposition is what makes such evidence meaningful.[22] Therefore, the problem of circularity is not really solved if Frame is advocating a consistent presuppositionalism.

The reason most apologists are uncomfortable with this approach is that its use of the transcendental argument is simply too comprehensive. Most do not like the idea of presupposing a system of belief as necessary to believing anything at all. Most apologetic methods use the concept of self-attestation, as Frame does, but they do not want to begin with the self-attesting Christ of Scripture. The reason for this has already been stated: The presuppositional scheme assumes that all facts are unintelligible outside the Christian system, which alone can account for them. Without Christ, all facts are brute, meaningless facts. Because of this, the facts actually become meaningful only after they are interpreted by the system. They do not stand on their own in any sense, which is why a direct appeal to facts is impossible. Given this situation, the Christian faith must be accepted on the basis of its rational adequacy to provide a structured and meaningful world.

How does the coherentism of presuppositionalism differ from other versions (e.g., Gordon Clark's)? Most significantly, the coherentism of presuppositionalism makes use of a transcendental argument that is comprehensive and seemingly unbreakable. In other words, the presuppositional critique of all other systems of non-Christian thought demon-

---

[22] Cf. Bahnsen, *Van Til's Apologetic*, 500. This is precisely one of the major points at issue between Bahnsen and Frame. Bahnsen faults Frame for advocating a direct appeal to facts, noting that Van Til believed that the argument for the Christian faith was necessarily indirect because of the dependence of facts upon a philosophy of fact.

A General Sampling of Apologetics III 79

strates the necessity of the triune God to meaningful predication, given the unintelligibility of facts within themselves. Does this make presuppositionalism an absolute proof for Christianity and absolutely compelling?

The answer to this question is both yes and no. The transcendental argument for Christianity put forth by presuppositionalists is absolutely compelling to those who think like Hegelians. There are many for whom transcendental coherence is absolutely compelling. They do not doubt the existence of facts, nor do they doubt that the facts have some meaning. What they believe differently from others, however, is that facts are meaningless without a comprehensive system to bring them into focus. To this kind of mentality, presuppositionalism will not only make sense; it will be the only apologetic that does.[23]

It is also inevitable that some will not consider the presuppositional argument an absolute proof. The type of circularity involved in the notion that "brute facts are mute facts" is simply unacceptable to many. Basil Mitchell describes this problem in terms of making a rational choice between scientific paradigms. Where strict proof is lacking, positions are often taken because one theory or the other allegedly explains the evidence best. It may be objected, however, that "certain 'basic presuppositions' or 'categorical frames' or 'conceptual schemes'... determine for each system what is to count as 'a fact' or 'evidence' and what are to be the criteria of rational acceptance." Thus, one scheme cannot claim superiority without begging the question, since what makes a theory more satisfactory, plausible, and faithful to the facts is precisely what is at issue.[24]

As Mitchell points out, when the system determines the facts, any appeal to evidence in support of the system is really pointless. After all, the

---

[23] It is interesting to note the radically different mentalities represented in the world of Christian apologetics. It almost seems as if evidentialists and classical apologists cannot even fathom the mentality of presuppositionalists. Much of the misunderstanding of presuppositionalism since its introduction in the 1930's has probably been due to the radically different mentalities of traditional apologists and presuppositionalists. Van Til was often faulted for his lack of clarity, but most of his writing is remarkably clear and easy to understand. Van Til's lack of clarity should be attributed mostly to his consistently presuppositional mindset, which has been shared by few Christians and even fewer Christian apologists.

[24] Basil Mitchell, *The Justification of Religious Belief* (New York: Oxford University Press, 1981), 75-76.

system is determining the evidence. For Van Til this would not be a problem, since his belief is built on the rational adequacy of his system. For those, however, who cannot gain certainty through rational adequacy alone, this becomes a serious problem. Evidences do not stand on their own and therefore provide no objective confirmation of belief. From this point of view, biblical and historical evidence for the Christian faith is really not evidence anymore; it is a logical entailment of one's system of belief. Even biblical testimony to miracles is of no value for the support of certainty, since on non-Christian assumptions miracles would be meaningless "monstrosities." Miracles are truly miracles only because miracles make sense within one's belief system.

The greatest problem arises, however, due to our living in a post-Kantian world. Kant proposed that the world of the mind does not necessarily correspond to the world-in-itself. Furthermore, we are daily confronted with those who have spun an imaginary world inside their heads that is quite different from our own. Even if we reject Kant, we cannot escape the temptation to wonder if the belief system in our minds really corresponds to the world outside.[25] Again, evidence is of no help in this because belief determines evidence.[26] Therefore, one is stuck with a ra-

---

[25] Could this have been the problem that Edward Carnell developed with Van Til's system? It is well known that Carnell suffered from severe depression and insomnia throughout his adult life. It is also known that depressive illness takes a severe toll on rational certainty. My personal belief is that Carnell's mental constitution was simply incompatible with Van Til's particular brand of coherentism. In short, Carnell had to find a basis for certainty outside his own head. It is also interesting that Carnell did his doctoral work on Kierkegaard. What was it in Kierkegaard that struck a responsive chord in Carnell? Could it be that Carnell, like Kierkegaard, was reacting against an imposing Hegelian mentality?

[26] The demand for a correspondence between facts and ideas is really at the heart of the complaints against Van Til's approach. Coherentists require only a single witness to truth, while others demand the dual witness of both coherence and correspondence. For rationalists, coherence is correspondence because the real is the rational. For empiricists, the rational is not always the real because of human fallibility and philosophical disagreements. Thus, the two tests must support and check each other, which they cannot do if the one is reduced to the other.

tional belief, the certainty of which is supported by its internal rational adequacy without external, objective support.[27]

In fact, Frame feels the force of this point. In opposition to his mentor, Frame openly admits that the transcendental argument is not absolutely compelling to all in the form in which Van Til offered it. A complete theistic argument requires more than proving that God provides an adequate basis for meaning and rationality. Van Til was "not sufficiently holistic" because the personality, attributes, and triunity of God require other arguments "of a more traditional kind." Frame also gives another reason why no single argument proves the entire doctrine of God: "To generalize: any argument can be questioned by someone who is not disposed to accept the conclusion." If no single argument guarantees persuasion, then "there is no argument that is immune to such additional questioning." Therefore, the transcendental argument is just one of many argument types required for a complete theistic proof.[28]

This is a remarkable statement coming from a presuppositionalist! In fact, Van Til himself would likely have considered it a major departure from his own system, a departure that compromises the heart of presuppositionalism. Even more interesting is Frame's point that the transcendental argument requires supplementation from other arguments of a more traditional kind. Is this a concession to traditional apologetics? Frame seems to recognize that the transcendental argument is not a purely rational argument after all. He obviously appreciates the force of the question previously put to Van Til: How can we know that the Christian God is necessary to account for the order of the world unless we have some experiential understanding of the world as orderly? Could this be the reason why he believes that the transcendental argument cannot stand

---

[27] Stating the problem this way may seem to downplay the role of the Holy Spirit in providing assurance. The Spirit, however, attests to the revelation of God in nature and in Scripture. If my belief system destroys the objectivity of God's revelation in nature, then the testimony of the Holy Spirit will be quenched, at least to some degree, through my errant way of thinking about it. In an unusual way, presuppositionalism has something in common with Barthianism at this point. Only those in Christ see God's revelation in nature. Barth denied the objectivity of natural revelation. Presuppositionalists do not, but it is arguable that their system logically entails such a denial.

[28] Frame, *Apologetics to the Glory of God*, 73.

alone? Arguments "of a more traditional kind" are based on our experience of the world. If by a direct appeal to facts we conclude that the world is structured in an orderly, rational, and causal way, then it makes sense to ask what kind of belief system is necessary to make sense of these things. Approached in this way, the transcendental argument becomes a powerful confirmation of Christianity, along with many other very powerful arguments of a traditional sort. This interpretation of Frame is confirmed by his criticism of Van Til in this regard:

> We have seen that Van Til is wrong to disavow direct arguments on the ground that they presuppose an autonomous understanding of the premises. A direct argument can, as easily as an indirect one, spring from the conviction that nothing is intelligible except through God.[29]

Interestingly, traditional apologists are doing precisely what Frame describes here: They argue from the phenomena of the world that God is necessary to account for them. Do such arguments pretend autonomy or neutrality, as Van Til argued? To this, we must answer no. In fact, traditional apologists have used transcendental arguments to justify the general reliability of sense experience, the principle of causality, and the laws of logic. Without these first principles predication is impossible. If Van Til can use a transcendental argument to justify the entire Christian system, then why criticize other apologists for using a transcendental argument to justify fundamental epistemological principles necessary to saying anything at all? We could go even further and say that without such principles, the objective revelation of God in nature and Scripture would not even be perceptible, since it comes to us through the senses.

Based on the problem of circularity described above, the direct argumentation advocated by Frame is really the only means of taking presuppositionalism beyond the narrow confines of a pure coherentism. Unless some epistemological essentials can be justified on the basis of their undeniablity, we can really never know from both reason and experience that the Christian worldview alone gives an adequate account of the objective world.[30] A pure coherentism keeps us locked inside our heads, which

---

[29] Ibid., 86.

[30] Van Til's response to this would be that first principles cannot be justified by their undeniability. Since neither chance nor impersonal law can account for them, it is also necessary to presuppose Christian theism in order to provide a complete justification for them. Traditional apolo-

will lead many to wonder whether the world really is the way we believe it to be. On this point of direct argumentation alone, Frame has taken presuppositionalism into the realm of traditional apologetics.

There is one other area in which Frame displays his affinity for traditional apologetics. The issue of probability marks a dividing line between presuppositionalism and most other approaches. Van Til criticized probabilistic approaches to apologetics as essentially giving the non-Christian an excuse for unbelief. If Romans 1:20 says that the truth of God's existence is so clearly revealed in nature that men are without excuse, then the Christian apologist dare not offer Christ as a mere probability. How could God, Van Til reasoned, condemn an individual for unbelief if his existence is only a probability?

Frame appreciates Van Til's point here but offers a different perspective. He does not wish to deny the objective clarity of God's revelation, but he wants to distinguish it from arguments that formalize it:

> I would also conclude that the word *probability* deserves to be rehabilitated in Reformed apologetics. We dare not concede that the evidence for God's existence or the justification for believing in God's existence is merely probable. To do that would be, as Van Til says, to deny the objective clarity of revelation. But to be honest we ought to admit that many of our arguments are only probable, if only because there is so much room for error in their formulation.[31]

---

gists come to discover the necessity of Christian theism through further application of first principles to the world, not by presupposing Christianity in the same way they assume first principles. The difference between Schaeffer and Van Til on this point provides a perfect example. Schaeffer's transcendental argument proceeds empirically to the conclusion that Christian theism is transcendentally necessary. Christianity is first proposed as a possible answer to the transcendental requirements of the world of our experience and then shown to be the only possible answer among the philosophic options. Schaeffer's approach (and Frame's) assumes some epistemological common ground with the non-Christian that makes his empirical argument possible. Van Til denies such common ground in experience and proceeds in a purely rational way. But at the very least, Van Til must assume a common rationality that makes the non-Christian's understanding of his argument possible. Both make use of first principles, but Van Til restricts himself to first principles of reason.

[31] Ibid., 86.

Frame recognizes, as most other apologists do, that there is often a disparity between the objectivity of God's truth and the subjective appropriation of that truth. Given the weaknesses and failings of human nature, it is often difficult to move from the certain revelation of God into subjective certainty. In fact, this is impossible on the basis of argument alone, the Holy Spirit being absolutely necessary for full conviction. Frame also realizes that an absolute proof for the Christian faith is not beyond rejection by the non-Christian, nor does it necessarily quell all doubts in the believer. Thus, for various reasons, the Christian apologist must have a place for probability in apologetics. Frame's explanation of probability is quite helpful:

> The logical probability of the truth of Christianity relative to its evidence is "1" or absolute certainty. But in the subjective sense, both the apologist and his hearers are often left with uncertainties because of inadequacies in the formulation of the argument and in our reception of it. And where there is suspicion of at least some legitimacy to uncertain reasoning, we may speak of some degree of probability.[32]

Most traditional apologists would not accept Frame's point that Christianity is absolutely certain. There is a sense, however, in which he makes this point in order to show the disparity that often exists between the objective evidence for Christianity and its subjective reception. A sound argument based on objectively certain evidence does not necessarily quell all doubts, especially if the hearer does not grasp the cogency of the argument. Human beings are not logic machines, their convictions naturally following the cogency of a sound argument. For many, a logical argument is not as powerful as a series of evidences that conspire together to justify faith for them. A confirmational or cumulative case approach is more powerful for some in creating strong faith than is a rationally sound argument. It is clear that Frame's point makes room for this, which is

---

[32] Ibid., 81-82n.28. The contrast between Frame and Ramm on this point is interesting. Whereas Frame believes that the objective evidence is certain and the subjective reception of some evidence may be probable, Bernard Ramm believes the objective evidence is probable and the subjective reception is certain by virtue of the witness of the Holy Spirit.

another reason why his particular expression of presuppositionalism should be accepted as a useful contribution to apologetics.[33]

That Frame has really bridged the gap between presuppositionalism and traditional apologetics should be clear to anyone who is familiar with Van Til's system. Even his point that the logical probability of Christianity relative to its evidence is "1" should be of no concern to those who think the case only probable. Most apologists would argue that the evidences for Christianity taken together make faith in Christ the only reasonable choice. If we believe Christianity to be the only reasonable choice, then certainly the probability of Christianity relative to its evidence is "1" practically and spiritually speaking, since there is no other option to which we may assign any remaining probability. For many, the cumulative case approach is meant to marshal as much evidence as is necessary to establish the truth of Christianity. Frame is really saying essentially the same thing. Since both fallible arguments and a direct perception of divine evidence are often sufficient and effective in bringing others to Christ, Frame's view of apologetics is practically congruent with the traditional approaches. What could make this clearer than his own statement that traditional apologetics represents a "presuppositionalism of the heart."[34]

---

[33] See Bahnsen, *Van Til's Apologetic*, 81-82n.104. Bahnsen criticizes Frame on his attempt to "rehabilitate" probability. Specifically, he faults Frame for making a distinction between evidence and argument in which the first is certain and the second is probable. This distinction, according to Bahnsen, vitiates the certainty of the evidence since it cannot receive more than a probable embodiment in an argument. The only way to avoid the force of Bahnsen's criticism is to affirm—as Frame does—that the certain evidence of God's revelation in nature and the self gets through to the heart either through the conscience or by some other means and thus holds the non-Christian without excuse. Arguments may or may not convey the certainty of divine evidence, but defects in human argument do not ultimately hinder the certain evidence that is daily conveyed by a revelational environment. Bahnsen simply allows for no disproportion between the certainty of evidence and the level of certainty conveyed by apologetic arguments. Frame believes that our apologetic arguments convey full certainty and eliminate the disproportion in principle but not always in practice. Sometimes our arguments are defective and sometimes their reception is defective, but the gospel still draws people to Christ.

[34] Frame, *Apologetics to the Glory of God*, 85.

Chapter 5

A GENERAL METHOD FOR APOLOGETICS

By previously sampling the better apologists of contemporary evangelicalism, the questions and options of argumentative apologetics have been systematically presented. This presentation, however, is only a first step toward a general theory of apologetics. While some areas of common belief began to surface through comparing and contrasting the major schools, the exposition seemed to turn up more disagreement than agreement. Indeed, many apologists would proceed no further in the attempt to develop a general theory, believing that the disagreements rule out the possibility altogether. In fact, there is another vantage point from which to view these disagreements; we may take what W.T. Jones calls "a meta-attitude toward philosophy."[1]

What Jones recommends is an analysis of philosophical disagreements and worldviews. The hypothesis he offers to account for philosophical disagreements is also applicable to apologetics, which is rooted in questions of epistemology and metaphysics. In attempting to get above or behind the disagreements of apologetics to an understanding of the precognitive orientations of the apologists themselves, it is possible to detect balanced orientations that will serve to mediate the conflicts among apologists. What Jones really offers is a theoretical approach to the precognitive issues underlying both philosophic and apologetic disagreements. At this level of analysis, a synthetic method begins to emerge, despite the seemingly unresolvable differences among apologists.

Precognitive issues, however, are only part of the problem. There are also cognitive issues that require attention. The differences among apologists concerning epistemological and metaphysical first principles reflect the traditional controversy over foundationalism and coherentism (contextualism). This controversy is also at the heart of the epistemic disagreements among evangelical apologists. While a great deal has been written about this complicated problem, the analysis of epistemic disa-

---

[1] Jones, "Philosophical Disagreements and World Views", 25.

greements from this perspective also suggests a balanced approach for resolving differences.

The operative word with respect to both the precognitive and cognitive issues of apologetics is *balance*. If apologetic options are really more like points on a continuum rather than discrete and unrelated positions, then it makes sense to seek for balanced and mediating positions to resolve disagreements. Apologetic disagreements have remained largely unresolved because few apologists have attempted to think about philosophy and apologetics this way. The principles of "hard logic" have prevailed in a field where the principles of "fuzzy logic" also have a place. There is a kind of discreteness to different apologetic positions, but all positions share some underlying resemblances. These resemblances are the key to providing a general theory to account for different apologetic theories.

A BALANCED APPROACH TO PRE-COGNITIVE ISSUES

While philosophical disagreements are often thought of in terms of differences on key philosophic issues, W.T. Jones points out that the source of such differences is due, in part, to non-cognitive factors. He argues that the solutions offered for a host of philosophical problems can be partly explained by differences in worldview. A worldview is a "configuration of cognitive and evaluative sets" similar to the "perceptual sets" that make different aspects noticeable or striking within the field of experience. Jones uses the example of hearing one's name stand out above the noise and babble of a party. These "sets" are among the factors that make a particular philosophic position seem plausible to some and implausible to others holding different cognitive and evaluative sets.[2]

It is important to stress Jones's point that precognitive orientations are "among the factors" that make a particular solution seem plausible and account for philosophical differences only "in part." He is not offering a genetic account of why philosophers hold the views they do, as if cognitive issues are no more than the result of differences in orientation and not also a cause. Apologetically speaking, this point is crucial for the same reason: The cognitive issues that separate apologists may not be reduced to differences in precognitive orientation but may also be discussed on their own merits. The kind of analysis Jones proposes could easily be misused to reduce philosophical and apologetical options to a form of

---

[2] Ibid., 24-25.

relativism based on differing personal tastes when it comes to worldviews. In the end, the precognitive orientations of the philosopher and apologist must submit to criticism and sound reasoning right along with the other factors that constitute a philosophic solution.

A Theory of Philosophical Disagreements

In the evaluation and interpretation of facts, philosophers and historians employ what Jones calls "cognitive and evaluative sets," or worldviews. In the case of a historical disagreement, historians will evaluate all statements pertaining to a particular historical event as confirmatory, neutral, or disconfirmatory. The problem is that historians do not order statements in the same way: "If we ask various historians to make a cut between those statements they regard as confirmatory and those they regard as neutral or disconfirmatory, we shall find that they make their cuts at different points."[3] Since no one is absolutely neutral, statements pertaining to a historical event will have a different "rank ordering" among historians. Historians may then be classified according to their evaluation of statements as either confirming or disconfirming an event: "I shall call any such rank ordering of sets from one extreme to the opposite extreme a *dimension*."[4] Each individual has a locus or location on the dimension in question, "his locus being inferable from where he cuts the events-array."[5]

These dimensions, which Jones also calls *orientations*, are as numerous as there are questions over which people differ. But perceptual sets and orientations are quite specific and limited. Historical sets are more "pervasive," but are still limited to specific questions of fact. Eventually, however, we arrive at "orientations sufficiently pervasive to be called world views." A worldview is a set or orientation so pervasive that it affects all of experience. Different philosophers reflect different loci or locations on each dimension, which accounts for their philosophical disagreements. Jones identifies three dimensions or orientations that are especially pervasive in analyzing common philosophical disagreements: (1) immediacy/mediation; (2) continuity/discreteness; (3) static/dynamic.[6]

---

[3] Ibid., 27.

[4] Ibid.

[5] Ibid., 28.

[6] Ibid., 28-29.

Jones begins by discussing the static/dynamic orientation because it is the easiest to understand. Put simply, "it is a range of possible attitudes towards change, from a set that selectively notices changes occurring in the environment to a set that selectively ignores or slights changes and focuses on what is unchanging or enduring." On a personal level, those with a strong static orientation notice the enduring aspects of experience, the constants, while those with a strong dynamic orientation tend to dislike stability and favor change. It is also possible to have one or the other orientation and yet "dislike those features of the experiential field that one's set (or orientation) brings into notice." Thus, one may have what Jones calls a positive or negative *cathexis* (feeling or attitude) with respect to one's orientation.[7]

Philosophically, the differences in orientation on this dimension are obvious. A strong static orientation leads to the idea that change is either illusory or paradoxical (Plato, Parmenides). A strong dynamic orientation leads in the opposite direction, making belief in fixity a problem that arises from a mere psychological need for security or certainty (Nietzsche, Dewey). Thus, philosophers see themselves living in a world of stable or unstable equilibrium or disequilibrium depending on their differences along this dimension.[8]

Apologetically, it is clear that categorical presuppositionalists are located toward the static extreme and metaphysical presuppositionalists are located toward the dynamic extreme. As one approaches the static extreme, the seeming holism of the dynamic extreme is viewed as evidence of the falsehood of this orientation, for the facts get lost without an "encapsulated and atomic" structure. Therefore, the static orientation becomes suspicious of the formality of neat systems that ignore the particularity of a discrete world. As one approaches the dynamic extreme, the atomism of the static extreme is viewed as evidence of the falsehood of this orientation, for the facts get lost by virtue of their isolation from each other. Therefore, the dynamic orientation becomes suspicious of systems that impose order on a discrete world.[9] In fact, Christian apologists do not

---

[7] Ibid., 29.

[8] Ibid., 30.

[9] While rationalists often accuse empiricists of failing to bring order out of the flux of disjointed facts, empiricists would be justified in accusing rationalists of failing to bring order out of the flux of conjoined facts. At either extreme, the Problem of the One and the Many cannot be solved;

occupy the extreme ends of this dimension, for all affirm both the static and the dynamic in experience to one degree or another. But differing locations on this and other dimensions have everything to do with how reason and sense experience are related in each apologetical system.

The continuity/discreteness dimension is concerned with our orientation to particulars in their relationship to one another. This dimension represents a range of orientations concerning unity and difference. Are differences among things a mere matter of degree, or is the world made up of "encapsulated entities" reflecting "sharp" lines of difference? Jones points to the difference between Hume's favorite metaphor and Hegel's as evidence of the crucial importance of this dimension. Hume viewed things as "loose and separate," like pool balls on a billiard table, and Hegel viewed things as unfolding like a flower from bud to blossom to fruit. Hume's philosophy clearly follows from his metaphor of loose and separate particulars, raising the problems of induction, the existence of the world, and the reality of the self. Jones says that "it never entered Hume's head to question the looseness and separateness of things from each other, for looseness and separateness are fundamental characteristics of his vision of the world." Thus, Hume denied or questioned what other philosophers took for granted.[10]

The "atomism" reflected in Hume is also evident in other modern philosophers, such as Wittgenstein and Russell, and may take either materialistic or logical forms. The holistic perspective of philosophers like Hegel is representative of the other extreme of this orientation. Jones shows that the respective metaphors of the two poles of this dimension are also suggestive of a link between this orientation and the static/dynamic vision described above. Just as Hume saw things as encapsulated and moved by outer forces, Hegel saw things as merging together and moving by inner forces. One can speak of the phases of bud, blossom, and fruit, but the phases reflect a continuous and unified inner-life. These metaphors sug-

---

whether facts are isolated or continuous, the end result is flux. Interestingly, the word *flux*, which means a continuous succession of changes, seems to apply as readily to the continuity extreme as to the discreteness extreme. And yet, rationalists like Clark and Carnell often use the word to describe the outworking of empiricism. The truth is that most Christian apologists avoid extreme expressions of both empiricism and rationalism because both fail to solve the One-and-Many problem.

[10] Ibid., 30-31.

gest that "discreteness-orientation and static-orientation form a standard configuration, or syndrome, and that continuity-orientation and dynamic-orientation form another configuration."[11]

These observations provide a simple and profound account of the main philosophical divisions of history. The two configurations of static/discreteness and dynamic/continuity involve separate truth tests appropriate to them. Some version of the correspondence theory is associated with the first, and some form of the coherence theory is associated with the second. Each configuration is an attempt to solve its own epistemological problem. In the case of the discreteness orientation, "the problem for philosophers with this vision of reality is how to get independently existing minds into correspondence with independently existing objects." In the case of the continuity orientation, "what now appears problematic is the existence of 'finite' minds . . . and finite truths. For both minds and truths are now perceived to exist only within the continuous texture of a single unity."[12] In the first orientation, thinking occurs *in* minds; in the second, thinking *is* mind.

Jones goes on to show the implications of his analysis in the areas of metaphysics, politics and logic. The infinite regress argument is a particular metaphysical case where differences of orientation make all the difference. If one begins with a vision of the world as continuous, encapsulated entities, then an infinite number of such entities must exist. If, on the other hand, one begins with a vision of the world as discrete entities, then the idea of linked, encapsulated entities becomes self-contradictory, and the idea of an infinite regress will be rejected. The idea of an infinite regress is really a conclusion presupposed in one's vision.[13]

Politically, thinkers with a discreteness orientation (Hobbes, Locke) favor a social contract theory stressing individual autonomy and rights. Thinkers with a continuity orientation (Burke, Hegel) view an explicit social contract as "merely the formal ratification of an underlying nexus of social relationships that have come into existence, not at a particular (discrete) moment in time, but gradually, by degrees, out of an immemo-

---

[11] Ibid., 30.

[12] Ibid., 31-32.

[13] Ibid., 32-33.

rial past."[14] Thus, respect for tradition and the historical continuity of political ideas is more pronounced in the continuity orientation.[15]

The two contrasting configurations also create disagreements in logic, especially when it comes to the nature of contradiction. The discreteness orientation affirms the consistent and the contradictory as discrete logical categories, and all assertions must go into one bucket or the other. For those oriented to continuity, the two categories or buckets are "not definitive and determinate but only tentative and provisional." Rather than being discrete categories, the two are in a "dynamic tension" that eventually resolves in a new conflict and tension. Therefore, progress is not a matter of sorting out truths from falsehoods (static/discreteness configuration) but of moving from one "unstable equilibrium to another" (dynamic/continuity configuration).[16]

The historic counterparts of these two visions are obvious, and the contemporary controversy over hard logic and fuzzy logic is clearly inspired by the differences between the two visions. Continuity logicians accuse their counterparts of oversimplifying and failing to represent the continuities they perceive. Discreteness logicians accuse their counterparts of muddle and confusion for "refusing to draw sharp distinctions." The difference between the two visions is well illustrated by Shopenhauer's criticism of the discreteness orientation:

> As Schopenhauer put it in a very revealing metaphor, a mosaic, no matter how small the bits of stone of which it is composed, always falsifies the continuous gradations of chiaroscuro that occur in nature and that are much more adequately represented by oil pigment on canvas.[17]

The third worldview orientation is that of immediacy/mediation. This vision interacts with and complicates the other two configurations. Some

---

[14] Ibid., 33.

[15] Respect for tradition and historical continuity in the area of theology is also affected by one's orientation. The close relationship between hierarchical church polity and doctrinal continuity in history is a reflection of the continuity orientation, while openness to self-government and the right of private conscience before God is a reflection of the discreteness orientation.

[16] Ibid., 33-34.

[17] Ibid.

philosophers reflect a preference "for what is at a distance, objective, and neutral," while others prefer "direct communion, empathy, and involvement." These two orientations correspond to two German terms describing experience "witnessed from outside" (*Erfahrung*) and experience that is "lived through" (*Erlebnis*). *Erfahrung* refers to knowledge about something and *Erlebnis* refers to knowledge by personal acquaintance.[18]

Jones points out that most people today probably take a middle position on this dimension. The relevance of this orientation is well illustrated by Kant:

> Kant's view is relatively mid-range, but tending toward the *Erfahrung* pole. His belief that concepts without percepts are empty and that percepts without concepts are blind asserts the need for both types of experience, but does so from outside, not from inside.[19]

Another way to characterize this orientation is to equate it with objectivity and subjectivity. In Kant's case, a "balanced" view is the goal, but in order to be "as impartial and disinterested as a judge," one must render a verdict from outside. Hence, Kant's tendency is to lean toward objectivity. Kierkegaard represents the opposite extreme, rejecting objectivity for complete subjectivity: "Kierkegaard started from a subjective commitment to subjective truth that wholly rejects objective truth as worthless."[20]

Another way to characterize this dimension is to distinguish feeling from formal proof. Subjective immediacy discounts verbalizations and proofs in favor of intuition based on metaphysical participation in the whole of reality. Even Kant's desire to limit reason in order to make room for faith is evidence of the tendency toward immediacy in modern philosophy. From this perspective, there is no such thing as "neutral objects and events over there outside us." Verbal descriptions of the world, if they are used, require "the language of poetry and mysticism, in which we express our insights and intuitions." In its extreme expressions, language fails completely because "the One is incommunicable, and everything else is an

---

[18] Ibid., 35.

[19] Ibid.

[20] Ibid., 36

illusion. Zen and the Via Negativa of Christian mysticism represent two otherwise different versions of this extreme position."[21]

This orientation is directly relevant to philosophy and apologetics because one's location on this dimension determines what constitutes making an adequate case. The *Erfahrung* (mediation) philosopher values evidence, arguments, and uncovering fallacious reasoning. But the *Erlebnis* (immediacy) philosopher appeals to aphorisms, epigrams, and riddles. The *Erlebnis* thinker does not lead us to a conclusion based on *outside* evidence; rather, we are led to see the world from *inside* his head through the power of shock and suggestion. The vision of each of these philosophers would lead each to view the other as making the "wrong sort of case."[22]

This point is the basis upon which apologists have recognized the need for an apologetic that appeals to those with a subjective orientation. John Warwick Montgomery affirms the relevance of a "responsible Subjective apologetic" for those who seek an answer "hidden in the Subjective depths of their own souls."[23] Most of contemporary evangelical apologetics, however, is not focused mainly on subjectivity because of a concern to establish the Christian faith as objectively true among many religious options. Most apologists take subjectivity quite seriously in their emphasis on the role of the Holy Spirit in persuasion. But there is also a concern for objectivity so that subjectivity may not be reduced to mere subjectivism.

Resolving Philosophical Disagreements

The tendency toward balanced orientations is not only wise; it is also practical. Jones explains the relevance of "mid-range" positions in a way that summarizes the rationale for this entire study. Philosophers of different schools "talk past" each other, unlike thinkers of the same school. Philosophers of the same school agree on what is problematic in experience and what constitutes evidence and making a proper case. But "mid-range" philosophers want to talk to their own school and those at both

---

[21] Ibid., 36-37.

[22] Ibid., 37.

[23] John W. Montgomery, "Introduction: The Apologists of Eucatastrophe," in *Myth Allegory and Gospel: An Interpretation of J.R.R. Tolkien/C.S. Lewis/G.K. Chesterton/Charles Williams*, ed. John W. Montgomery (John W. Montgomery, 1974), 20.

extremes. Mid-range thinkers require "synthesis and compromise," since some truth is usually found on both sides of an issue.[24]

In actuality, most of evangelical apologetics is somewhere near a mid-range position on all three dimensions. There are extremes, of course, but these are really the exception and not the rule. There are also cognitive factors involved in apologetic disagreements, but the main problem is that most apologists have not sought *convergence* because they have not *wanted* to do so. "Synthesis and compromise" have not been a necessary requirement perhaps because most apologists adopt a discreteness orientation when it comes to their own personal systems. The desire for originality and personal and professional distinction may also have something to do with the fact that major Christian apologists are often reluctant to admit that there is "something to be said for both sides." The party spirit often quenches the spirit of unity that should characterize those who are working for the salvation of the world in Christ. In the end, an apologetic of universal appeal is better than an apologetic that appeals to novelty or originality.

Balanced perspectives that gravitate toward the mid-range are justified because the orientations themselves arise from our experience of reality. They are not merely arbitrary choices about what to perceive and how to reason; experience itself suggests these dimensional continua, and careful reflection is required to determine where to stand on them in order to do justice to the truth. Conflicts arise in two situations: (1) Extreme positions are taken consistently across dimensions; (2) Opposite positions are taken on two dimensions. Jones explains how a conflict of this second kind produced a "strainful type of configuration" in Descartes' philosophy.

By combining the discreteness and immediacy orientations, Descartes set up a conflict between being in the world without being a part of it (discreteness) but wanting to be a part of it (immediacy). The strong discreteness orientation is especially evident in Descartes' strict separation between soul and body, as well as in other views that reflect this underlying orientation: "All relations are external in the sense that if any one entity (a soul, a moment, an object) were withdrawn from the whole set of entities comprising the universe, everything else would remain exactly what it was before, unchanged."[25]

---

[24] Jones, "Philosophical Disagreements and World Views", 38.

[25] Ibid., 40.

In order to feel like a part of this discrete world, Descartes referred everything to God. God not only overcomes the insecurity and uncertainty of the discreteness orientation, but he also guarantees the existence of the world and the correlation between the world and our ideas about it. Jones notes that all this "puts a heavy burden on God." In fact, those philosophers who share Descartes' configuration without accepting his solution find themselves saddled with a feeling of alienation and the "existential problem of coming to terms, personally, with this vision of the world."[26]

Jones offers a second example of this same conflict as it played itself out in the thinking of Wittgenstein. In a consistent discreteness/mediation configuration, language is the bridge or link between the discrete entities of the world and the individual mind. Since the real entities out there are viewed as "encapsulated and atomic, the philosopher will derogate ordinary language and aim at constructing an ideal language that is adequate for reporting about the nature and inter-relations of these atomic facts." Language is not viewed as "a barrier that separates him from reality. On the contrary, being content to stay on the outside, he expects and wants some mediating instrument."[27]

For Wittgenstein, however, language became a problem because of his immediacy orientation: "Now language is perceived as a barrier to be overcome, a veil to be torn aside, so that the philosopher can experience the world immediately, i.e., as it really is, undistorted by language." While other language philosophers would consider the pursuit of an ideal language possible and desirable, Wittgenstein was led by his immediacy orientation "to suspect that this undertaking is vain." Instead, there must be something beyond the most ideal language that is "unspeakable," "das Mystische," and "that cannot be put into words." As Jones points out, such passages in Wittgenstein "tend to be passed over, as a kind of embarrassment, by philosophers whose discreteness vision of the world is not complicated by *Erlebnis*-orientation."[28]

---

[26] Ibid. Had Descartes taken a mid-range position with respect to the discreteness/continuity and immediacy/mediation orientations, God would not have had to bear the burden of his extreme discreteness worldview. God would still play a role, but not that of resolving a severe dialectical tension. Dialectical philosophies and theologies are all characterized by this kind of worldview conflict.

[27] Ibid., 40-41.

[28] Ibid., 41.

It is also possible to observe this type of conflict in apologists. Van Til embraced a strained configuration by combining the continuity and static orientations. His tendency toward the continuity extreme accounts for his belief that individual facts cannot speak, even to reveal their own preconditions. Without pre-interpretation by special revelation, one cannot distinguish a single fact from another. Van Til's example of the man of water attempting to climb out of the water on a ladder made of water is obvious proof of his extreme continuity orientation.[29] In this example, one cannot even distinguish the man, the ladder, or the watery medium because all is undifferentiated oneness without God's interpretation.

There is, however, a conflict in Van Til with respect to orientations. He is also committed to the static interpretation of reality because general revelation implies that facts are distinguishable and atomic by virtue of their creation and interpretation by God. Therefore, something must overcome the monism of continuity to encapsulate the facts. This is where the Christian system comes in; by its light, the clear, watery medium becomes a world on dry land. Just as Descartes used God to bear the load of his orientational conflict, so Van Til does the same. Most apologists, however, find Van Til's solution to the conflict no more satisfying than most philosophers found Descartes' solution. Ironically, even though Van Til was the enemy of dialecticism in philosophy and theology, his own perspective was also dialectical at the pre-cognitive level.

How can the strain of conflicting orientations be removed? Jones's answer would be to bring them into balance. By moderating the discreteness orientation, Descartes would have been able to see God in the particulars and their relationships, since the logical relationships among the facts would not be erased by their extreme discreteness. Also, by balancing discreteness and continuity, God does not bear the entire burden for the logical relationships among the facts of the world. The facts also reveal a continuity that is confirmed by reason and revelation.

This solution would also have taken much of the pressure off of Wittgenstein. By moderating the immediacy orientation, he would have been able to see that the mediation of the meaning of facts to the mind through

---

[29] Van Til, *Defense of the Faith*, 119. Even though Van Til uses this illustration as an example of the non-Christian's methodology, it does represent for him the true epistemological state of affairs without the presupposition of Christian theism. The central problem for the non-Christian is also the central problem for the Christian.

language does not necessarily distort the world in our understanding. Indeed, by accepting mediation as a normal part of epistemology, Wittgenstein would not have discredited language because it separates us from reality. Accepting mediation implies our belief that a perfect, complete, and immediate knowledge of reality is both impossible and unnecessary. Discrete objects and minds are not totally separate just because they are not plugged into each other. Wittgenstein's error was that he conceived of discreteness and continuity as an either/or proposition instead of a both/and proposition. In the end, the binary logic of his discreteness orientation short-circuited his philosophy of language.

A balanced orientation would also have saved Van Til a great deal of controversy and criticism. Had he moderated his continuity orientation, he would not have rejected all common ground on the basis of the problematics of an idealist epistemology. Like Wittgenstein, he opted for an either/or approach to discreteness and continuity, and chose continuity as the basis from which to launch a transcendental coherentism.

What Jones's analysis shows is that balanced orientations must accomplish two things: (1) The mind must be brought into contact with particulars, (2) The particulars must also be rational in order to be intelligible. Put another way, the truth is both correspondent and coherent.[30] Where truth is defined in terms of either but not both of these standards, a dimensional imbalance can be detected. While many apologists have acknowledged both of these standards, no attempt has been made to analyze why there is still no agreement on the subject of truth among evangelicals.

A general theory of apologetics requires both coherence and correspondence as mutually supportive standards in the justification of knowledge, and W.T. Jones shows why this must be so: *The only alternative to balanced orientations is dialectical tensions in which conflicting orientations war against each other, even within the same philosophical position.* Dialectical tensions also reveal internal contradictions. Internal consistency and orientational balance are roughly proportional to each other. Thus, balance is not merely an aesthetic or psychological goal; it is directly related to the internal logic of a set of beliefs.

---

[30] See Adler, *Intellect*, 98. Adler points out that these two are the only major theories of truth in the history of Western thought, each with minor variations.

A BALANCED APPROACH TO COGNITIVE ISSUES

Disagreements about the justification of belief have an obvious impact on apologetic methodology. Controversies over appropriate theories of truth are related to differences concerning the logic or structure of epistemic justification. What is the relationship between truth and justification in epistemology? Geisler and Feinberg explain:

> Truth and justification can be seen to be different concepts in that someone may be justified in believing some proposition p but p may in fact be false. Similarly, one could be justified in believing p, and yet we could deny that he *knew* p, since p is false. In other words, justification is a necessary condition of a belief being true and counting as knowledge, but it is not alone a sufficient condition.[31]

This distinction between truth and justification may be understood according to the traditional distinction between metaphysics and epistemology. Metaphysics is concerned with what is real and epistemology is concerned with how we know. The goal of truth is to come to knowledge of what is real, whereas the goal of justification is to determine the method by which such knowledge may be attained. Clearly, what we know (truth) is closely related to how we know (justification), but the two terms have a different focus. Just as an argument may have both formal validity and a false conclusion, so a belief may be both justified and yet false. For this reason, logicians stress the importance of both valid form and true premises in framing a sound argument.

Theories of truth and theories of justification are similarly related. Coherence and correspondence are tests for truth, but each of these tests involves an underlying theory of justification. Theories of truth tell us that what is real coheres and/or corresponds to reality; theories of justification tell us how these tests work and why they work. Like validity, they are concerned with the epistemic *structure* of beliefs, not the truth or falsity of any specific belief.[32]

---

[31] Norman L. Geisler and Paul D. Feinberg, *Introduction to Philosophy: A Christian Perspective* (Grand Rapids: Baker Book House, 1980), 151.

[32] In stressing the connections among precognitive orientations, truth tests, and theories of justification, it is important to observe that the connections are not always parallel. For example, a philosopher like

A Theory of Epistemic Disagreements

Foundationalism and coherentism (contextualism) are the two "logics or structures of epistemic justification."[33] Foundationalism has been the majority view throughout history: "Foundationalism is the view that there is a structure of knowledge whose foundations, though they support all the rest, are themselves in need of no support. Epistemic justification, then is pyramidal." The main point here is that while beliefs in the "higher tiers" of the pyramid are justified by beliefs (propositions) in the "lower tiers," the lowest foundational beliefs require no rational justification.[34]

Knowledge, then, is built up from *directly* justified, or epistemologically basic, beliefs. Non-basic beliefs are *indirectly* justified. A number of criticisms have been leveled against foundationalism and the idea of immediately justified beliefs. Critics doubt that any basic beliefs exist or that enough could be agreed upon to serve as a foundation for knowledge. For what statements could possibly serve as *incorrigible* or *indubitable* foundations for knowledge? Another criticism is that foundationalism leads either to an infinite regress of justification or to dogmatism concerning foundational beliefs. Each lower belief in the pyramid demands justification if it is to be grounded. But in order to avoid an infinite regress, we must exempt basic beliefs from the evidential requirement of all other beliefs and dogmatically accept them as self-evident. Thus, the grounded beliefs are supported by seemingly ungrounded beliefs.

For those who find foundationalism unacceptable, coherentism seems to be the only other rational alternative. This view is also called *contextualism* because of the idea that facts gain their meaning from the interpretive context in which they are placed. Coherentism is the view that a belief is justified by its relationship to other beliefs within a web or network of beliefs. Thus, there are no foundational, basic, or bedrock beliefs.[35]

Gordon Clark might advocate a coherence theory of truth and a foundationalist theory of justification. Another philosopher like Hilary Putnam might be closer to a correspondence theory of truth while advocating a coherence theory of justification.

[33] Ibid., 152.

[34] Ibid.

[35] Ibid., 161.

Thomas Kuhn and Willard Quine have made this theory of justification popular.[36-37] Since all facts are *theory-laden*, it is impossible to arrive at immediately justified beliefs. Coherentism, however, does not avoid the problems of foundationalism, for it also leads to an infinite regress of justification. But the coherentist hopes to avoid this problem by giving reasons "three or four steps down the chain of justification." Whereas the foundationalist begins with a basic belief, the coherentist begins with a basic standard of sufficient evidence in terms of multiple reasons.

Of course, if one goes back only three or four links in the chain, one can also ask for reasons for the first of those links, and so one *ad infinitum*. There is also a sense in which the coherentist's theory of justification hangs in the air, since it never rests on a foundation of self-evident beliefs. Since all that is required is a coherent system of beliefs, it is possible to construct internally coherent worldviews on the basis of this theory that bear no resemblance to reality or to other equally coherent visions of the world. The implication that coherentism leads to relativism seems to follow from the problems above, and philosophers like Quine are not ashamed to draw this conclusion. Other coherentists who lean more toward a correspondence theory of truth deny the separation between the world and our ideas since "theory and experience interpenetrate."[38] In other words, theory and experience support and check each other so that one's theory of reality remains anchored in the facts. Of course, this approach raises the question of how we know the facts in order to know that our theory corresponds to them.

While others like John Meadors have written in greater detail about the relevance of this controversy to apologetics, the purpose of this study is to determine whether or not a balanced solution to the problem of epistemic justification is available.[39] Is there a balanced approach to this issue that does justice to each side of the controversy and provides good

---

[36] Thomas S. Kuhn, *The Structure of Scientific Revolutions*, 2nd ed. (Chicago: University of Chicago Press, 1970).

[37] Willard V.O. Quine, *From a Logical Point of View*, 2nd ed. (New York: Harper & Row Publishers, 1953).

[38] Geisler and Feinberg, *Introduction to Philosophy*, 163.

[39] John Thomas Meadors, *The Foundationalist Debate and Contemporary Christian Apologetics*. Ph.D. diss, The Southern Baptist Theological Seminary, 1993.

and sufficient answers to the problems raised above? The following proposal argues in favor of an affirmative answer to this question based on recent scholarly contributions.

Resolving Epistemic Disagreements

A balanced position must resolve two problems raised above: (1) The disagreement over foundational first principles and coherence as a structure for epistemic justification; (2) The unacceptable alternatives of an infinite regress, dogmatism, and ultimately baseless beliefs. While these are significant problems, a number of competent philosophers and apologists have proposed some well-reasoned answers.

The disagreement over foundational first principles and coherence is the easier of the two problems to resolve. Controversies are often aggravated by the assumption that two opposing approaches are incompatible when, in fact, they are not. By attaching an *ism* to each pole of the controversy, the assumption of incompatibility is built into the issue from the outset. In fact, foundationalism and coherentism are not so far apart. They not only share most of the same problems, but they share the principle of coherence in common. As Norman Geisler points out, "Even coherentism uses the first principle of contradiction to test the coherence of its system."[40] The main difference between the two camps is not opposing principles of justification but the number of principles. Geisler, for example, lists twelve first principles as opposed to the coherentist's single principle.

The coherentist faces the same problem with a single principle that the foundationalist faces with many: How do we justify the principles by which we justify beliefs? By focusing on a single principle of justification, the coherentist avoids the problem of having to justify Geisler's eleven other principles. And certainly, coherence is likely the one principle most would accept as an undisputed first principle. But one principle has the same burden to bear as many principles. Therefore, if one is able to justify coherence as a first principle, one is also likely to be able to justify other first principles in the same way. Thus, both foundationalism and coherentism must justify one or more first principles. In this respect, the con-

---

[40] Norman Geisler, "First Principles," in *Encyclopedia of Christian Apologetics*, 250.

troversy may be reduced to the central problem of foundationalism, which is the justification of first principles.[41]

Based on this understanding of the controversy, both approaches are left to solve the second problem of an infinite regress, dogmatism, and baseless beliefs. If this can be done, the question of the correct number of first principles will virtually resolve itself. At the very least, we may say at this point that foundationalism represents the more comprehensive approach, and it includes the first principle of coherentism, namely, the principle of contradiction. In this respect, it has a greater appeal to the Christian apologist because it provides greater resources for the justification of knowledge. But in the end, if foundationalism cannot be justified, then coherentism will be left without justification as well. Epistemic justification is really what is at stake, not just foundationalism. Therefore, the focus from here on will be more on the justification of first principles than the controversy between foundationalists and coherentists.

The manner in which first principles are held has everything to do with modern attacks on foundationalism. In an impressive article against foundationalism, Richard Topping critiques the apologetic strategies of Carl Henry and Stuart Hackett.[42] What is especially important in this article is the manner in which Topping states the problem of these two apologists: "Can the foundation that they each propose provide enough or any indubitable and non-inferential propositions from or upon which Christian faith and theology can be consistently justified?"[43] The words *indubitable* and *incorrigible* are used repeatedly throughout this article to describe foundational first principles. The problem here is that Topping assumes the classical foundationalism of Descartes as the basis of his critique, despite the fact that evangelical foundationalists rarely commend first principles as indubitable.

---

[41] At bottom, coherentism is just an attenuated foundationalism. By focusing justification on a web of beliefs, the coherentist has pushed the problem of justifying his first principle into the background while keeping the *application* of his first principle in the foreground. Foundationalists, on the other hand, have kept the *justification* of first principles in the foreground, recognizing that the *application* of first principles is meaningless without their prior justification.

[42] Richard R. Topping, "The Anti-Foundationalist Challenge to Evangelical Apologetics," *The Evangelical Quarterly* 63, no. 1 (1991), 45-60.

[43] Ibid., 46.

Evangelical foundationalists like Geisler speak of first principles as *undeniable* rather than as *indubitable* partly because they appreciate Topping's problem with Cartesian foundationalism:

> The recognition that logical laws are constructs based on limited and fallible human experience and that future theoretical innovations may, as they have in the past, require that they be modified to account for these innovations loosens the ineluctable grip of so-called *a priori* logical laws.[44]

Topping's point, if correct, may loosen the grip of *a priori* logical laws, but it does not overturn the reasons offered to support them. Though first principles may be doubted, it is true that their use is required even to discredit them. In other words, they are *undeniable* even if they are not *indubitable*.[45] First principles do not require an iron grip in order to serve as necessary tools of justification. On the basis of Topping's own criterion of justification through sufficient reasons, it is possible to argue that there is "reason enough" for their use.

Topping's analysis of the foundationalist quest leads to an unnecessary dichotomy between giving reasons and tracing causal relations. Topping argues that Kant and a number of other Western philosophers switched metaphors with regard to offering sufficient justification. Instead of sticking to the idea that justification is a matter of giving reasons, many philosophers employ the metaphor of "visual perception." Since visual perception traces causal relations, these philosophers conceive of justification as tracking the cause of a higher belief through lower beliefs to a bedrock belief. This switch supposedly moves justification from the "logical space of reasons" to the physical space of cause and effect inspired by the visual metaphor.[46]

At best, all Topping's observation shows is that it is possible to distinguish giving reasons from tracing causal relations, and there are certainly good reasons to view reason and causality as related in our experience. A chain of reasoning is very much like a chain of events; indeed, the comprehensibility of a series of related events requires a correlation between

---

[44] Ibid., 55.

[45] See Adler, *Intellect*, 155. Adler also refers to first principles as undeniable.

[46] Ibid., 58.

reason and causality.⁴⁷ How is the "logical space of reasons" *left* for the "domain of causal relations" when the two are clearly related in experience? The distinction between the two domains merely makes it possible to doubt a connection between them, and Topping has not given *reason enough* to view this distinction as a true dichotomy.⁴⁸ Furthermore, Topping has failed to give an account of the principle of contradiction that drives his own coherentist theory of justification. By focusing attention on the problems of classical foundationalism, he has diverted attention from the fact that his own view shares the foundationalist's "Cartesian anxiety," demanding as it does an account of at least one first principle.⁴⁹

A number of Christian philosophers have addressed the problems of classical foundationalism and proposed modifications in line with Topping's legitimate criticism. William Alston's well known article in *The Journal of Philosophy* defends a simple foundationalism that is non-dogmatic with respect to foundations.⁵⁰ Alston's contention is that "for

---

⁴⁷ See Geisler, "Sufficient Reason, Principle of," in *Encyclopedia of Christian Apologetics*, 712. The principle of sufficient reason is possibly the best illustration of the relationship between reason and causality. While Geisler would argue that the principle of causality avoids the contradictions and agnosticism that result from a consistent application of the principle of sufficient reason, even the principle of causality implies a correlation between reason and causality that seems absolutely necessary to explanation. Jones's analysis is relevant here. Topping's discreteness orientation appears to drive a wedge between the logical space of reasons and the domain of causal relations, whereas a balanced orientation would preserve more continuity between the two. Ironically, Topping shares Descartes' orientational conflict and merely proposes coherentism rather than God as the solution to it. The result, however, is a strained configuration owing to the unresolved tension between reasons and causal relations.

⁴⁸ See Richard J. Bernstein, *Beyond Objectivism and Relativism: Science, Hermeneutics, and Praxis* (Philadelphia: University of Pennsylvania Press, 1983), 16-25. Descartes encouraged what has become perhaps the greatest temptation of modern philosophy: Since I can doubt, I should doubt. The capacity to doubt the relationship between subject and object does not carry with it the grounds for doing so. This mistake might be labeled the Doubter's Fallacy.

⁴⁹ Ibid., 59.

⁵⁰ William P. Alston, "Two Types of Foundationalism," *The Journal of Philosophy* 73, no. 7 (April 8, 1976), 165-185.

any immediately justified belief that one has, one can find adequate reasons for the proposition that one is so justified." He explains how this works:

> Though the simple foundationalist requires *some* immediately justified beliefs in order to terminate the regress of justification, his position permits him to recognize that all epistemic beliefs require mediate justification. Therefore, for any belief that one is immediately justified in believing, one *may* find adequate reasons for accepting the proposition that one is so justified.[51]

Alston is saying that a lower-level basic belief may be justified by a higher-level epistemic belief or principle, thus removing the stigma of dogmatism from basic beliefs. Throughout this discussion, the higher-level epistemic belief is also called a meta-belief, a higher-level correlate, or a higher-level doxastic correlate. What makes it "higher-level" is that such beliefs require reasons whereas a "lower-level" belief is basic. This view really combines the logic of foundationalism with the logic of coherentism. It recognizes the pyramidal structure of beliefs but also recognizes the importance of higher-level meta-beliefs that provide a mediate justification for lower-level basic beliefs. This is meant to satisfy the coherentist's concern that all beliefs be supported by other reasons.[52]

Alston provides a concise summary of a sound and influential approach that does justice to the problems of foundationalism, satisfies the concerns of the coherentist, and meets the requirement of accounting for first principles:

> But the point is that the simple foundationalist need not, any more than the coherence theorist, mark out certain points at which the regress of showing *must* come to an end. He allows the possibility of one's giving reasons for an assertion whenever it is appropriate to do so, even if that assertion is of a foundation.[53]

This, it would seem, is truly the best of both worlds in the area of epistemic justification. Michael Czapkay Sudduth is an impressive scholar who has recognized the value of Alston's proposals and has extended their

---

[51] Ibid., 183.

[52] Ibid., 183-184.

[53] Ibid., 185.

application to Reformed epistemology and apologetics.[54-55] Czapkay Sudduth uses the epistemology of Alston to demonstrate the "compatibility of Reformed epistemology and evidentialism." He calls his approach *Higher-Level* or *Bi-Level Evidentialism*. His approach translates Alston's logic of epistemic levels to Reformed epistemology by imposing an "evidentialist requirement for the justification of any higher-level belief about the epistemic status" of a generally accepted belief. This idea, he claims, is compatible with the "central claims" of Reformed epistemology and satisfies the evidentialist's desire for "reflective rationality."[56]

Czapkay Sudduth's approach assumes a "modest foundationalism," which is defended by Alston and Plantinga and distinguishes between epistemic levels.[57] Like Alston, Czapkay Sudduth agrees that even an immediately justified belief may be assessed in terms of *reasons*. Thus, a lower-level basic belief is *supported* by the mediate justification of higher-level beliefs and by the existence of a "valid epistemic principle that relates to the belief in question."[58] He illuminates this point by distinguishing between "the *supports-relation* and the *basis-relation* in a noetic structure," which implies that "having adequate grounds for the belief that p (and hence having a justification) is independent of believing that p." This makes it possible for a belief to be truly basic and yet be supported by

---

[54] Michael L. Czapkay Sudduth, "Bi-Level Evidentialism and Reformed Apologetics," *Faith and Philosophy* 11, no. 3 (July 1994): 379-396.

[55] Michael L. Czapkay Sudduth, "Prospects for 'Mediate' Natural Theology in John Calvin," *Religious Studies* 31 (Mar 1995): 53-68. See also Michael L. Czapkay Sudduth, "Calvin, Plantinga, and the Natural Knowledge of God: A Response to Beversluis," *Faith and Philosophy* 15, no. 1 (1998): 92-103.

[56] Michael L. Czapkay Sudduth, "Alstonian Foundationalism and Higher-Level Theistic Evidentialism," *International Journal for Philosophy of Religion* 37 (F 1995): 25.

[57] Ibid., 31.

[58] Ibid., 32. The author gives some examples of these higher-level epistemic correlates as follows: S's belief that a given belief is rational, justified (immediately or mediately), formed in a reliable manner, or based on adequate grounds. As a specific example, the principle of undeniability could be offered as a reason for the higher-level belief that first principles are immediately justified and therefore self-evident.

A General Method for Apologetics

other items in the noetic structure. "Reflective rationality," then, means that being justified is not simply a matter of *being* in a "good cognitive state" with respect to a particular belief, but the believing subject must be *aware* of being in such a state. This is important because "our idea of justification has developed within the social context of answering objections to our beliefs." This, in turn, leads to two evidentialist requirements:

> (1) a *maximal requirement* that individuals themselves have good reasons for a belief, especially if that belief is the type of belief which is subject to doubt by large segments of society, and (2) a *minimal requirement* that there is evidence somewhere in the community for a belief.[59] (emphasis mine)

The emphasis on reflective rationality by traditional evidentialists is good, but they fail to make an important distinction:

> Where traditional evidentialism goes wrong is in its failure to distinguish between *reflective* (second-order) and *unreflective* (first-order) rationality or justification. The goal of critical reflection on our beliefs is an important aim, but it should not be confused with the first-order goal of securing true beliefs, or at least of being in a strong position with respect to acquiring true beliefs.[60]

The point here is that one may be justified in having certain beliefs because those beliefs are rational, even if they are not reflectively rational. At the lower level, people acquire many true beliefs for which they do not (and often cannot) offer reasons. Reflective rationality, however, requires justified belief in the adequacy of the grounds of belief. In this way, Czapkay Sudduth shows the compatibility of higher-level evidentialism with a moderate foundationalism.

Czapkay Sudduth puts this powerful approach to work mediating conflicts in apologetics. In "Bi-Level Evidentialism and Reformed Apologetics," the author constructs "an alternative apologetic system which subsumes the elements of positive value in both presuppositionalism and evidentialism while avoiding their respective errors."[61] The relevance of this article to the goal of this study is obvious: Evidentialism and presup-

---

[59] Ibid., 37-38.

[60] Ibid., 38.

[61] Czapkay Sudduth, "Bi-Level Evidentialism," 379.

positionalism represent the two extreme ends of the spectrum of argumentative apologetics; if, therefore, a system exists that subsumes the positive elements of both, such a system will be extremely valuable in developing a general theory of apologetics. The difference between the two extremes is really a difference concerning first principles.

On the one hand, presuppositionalists argue that it is "epistemically appropriate" to start with a belief in God and Scripture, since every system begins with assumed premises and ends in first principles. Since these premises and principles are properly "argued *from*, never *to*, there is no need to prove the existence of God or that Scripture is His Word." Also, since these Christian beliefs are produced by the regenerating work of the Holy Spirit, it makes no sense to offer apologetic arguments for them. Such beliefs might be called "privileged" beliefs because only the regenerate believer has access to them. On the other hand, evidentialists do not object to using Christian belief as a first principle, but they do object to the idea that such beliefs need not be established by argument. Intuitive truths and first principles must be argued *to*, never *from*.[62]

Based on the previous elaboration of Bi-Level Evidentialism, it is possible to predict Czapkay Sudduth's course in solving this problem. Since his approach provides for both basic beliefs and evidential requirements at the epistemic level, "Bi-Level Evidentialism allows the Reformed thinker to enter into the task of 'giving a reason for the hope that is within him,' even when that hope is a product of, what John Calvin called, the *testimonium Spiritus Sancti*."[63]

The testimony of the Holy Spirit obviously creates a special problem for the presuppositional apologist. Since Christian belief requires the testimony of the Holy Spirit, the non-Christian has no access to the reasons for such belief. In other words, the epistemic function of the Holy Spirit in belief formation implies that at least some Christian beliefs are privileged, which implies that they cannot be rationally defended. And since the defense of a minimal theism is not the concern of presuppositionalists, they face the dilemma of having to defend what on their principles cannot be defended.

Czapkay Sudduth refers to this "subset" of Christian beliefs as *privileged epistemic state* beliefs (PES-beliefs) as opposed to *theistic* beliefs

---

[62] Ibid., 382, 387.

[63] Ibid., 393.

(Pt-beliefs) and further explains the dilemma of presuppositionalists. Since apologetics must *show* the "positive epistemic status" of the Christian belief system, the apologist must provide "audience-relative" reasons that provide adequate justification. Such reasons are available if one is offering reasons for theistic beliefs (Pt-beliefs), but privileged beliefs (PES-beliefs) are another matter, since these require epistemic conditions accessible only to the Christian. How, then, can discursive support be offered in order to *show* them to those lacking the Christian experience? In short, how does one move from mediately justified Pt-beliefs to immediately justified PES-beliefs?[64]

By taking the higher-level evidentialist option this dilemma may be overcome. The apparatus of epistemic level distinctions allows the apologist to rise above immediately justified PES-beliefs to "the justificatory conditions of the higher-level epistemic correlates," which are not privileged and therefore accessible to the non-Christian.[65] This option may be summarized in the following principle:

> Given any person S, if S's belief that Pc (where Pc = any Christian belief) is either (a) immediately justified, (b) mediately justified, or (c) both [(a) and (b)], and if p is either (a) or (b) then the correlative epistemic belief that **Pc*** is justified *only if* **Pc*** is based upon adequate reasons.[66]

This approach combines both a moderate evidentialism with respect to lower-level beliefs and a strong evidentialism with respect to higher-level beliefs. It also provides a solid basis for positive apologetics, which is necessary because a purely negative apologetic is inadequate. Recognizing their apologetic dilemma, presuppositionalists have resorted to a negative approach to apologetics that merely addresses objections against Christianity. While they can show the coherence of a set of Christian doctrines, coherence alone does not show that a set of propositions is true: "Coherence is not a truth-conducive mode of justification." But by employing a Bi-Level Evidentialism, presuppositionalists may also engage in positive apologetics.[67]

---

[64] Ibid., 387.

[65] Ibid., 389.

[66] Ibid., 391.

[67] Ibid., 387.

A general method of apologetics requires balanced worldview orientations and an expression of foundationalism that provides an adequate structure of justification. W.T. Jones and William Alston have provided an understanding of these components. Michael Czapkay Sudduth has shown how the first steps might be taken to resolve some difficult problems in apologetics. The next step is to summarize contemporary evangelical apologetics in light of the method developed thus far.

If the apologists and apologetic schools discussed in the previous chapters are viewed in light of balanced worldview orientations and Bi-Level Evidentialism, an apologetic synthesis is possible. Of course, the desired synthesis will not validate all the details of each approach. Additional criticism will be necessary to reshape the edges of each school slightly in order to fit each piece of the puzzle into a single apologetic methodology. Once this is done, the differences among the schools will appear as perspectival differences among otherwise compatible perspectives. The end result will be an apologetic of tremendous resources and the flexibility to make contact with the multiple perspectives of the modern mind.

CHAPTER 6

A GENERAL SUMMARY OF APOLOGETICS

Before proceeding to the summary and analysis of apologetics, it will be helpful to review the steps taken so far and their purpose in bringing the study to this point. First, a detailed presentation of contemporary evangelical apologetics was offered as a basis to develop a general theory of apologetics. In order to arrive at an accurate representative sampling of the field, Stuart Hackett's analysis of argumentative apologetics was employed to help guide in the selection and elaboration of the major approaches. By focusing on important representatives of each school, it is possible to abstract the issues and alternatives of apologetics so that they may be systematically summarized. An accurate synopsis is required for a correct analysis, and a correct analysis is required for an apologetic synthesis. Many suggestions as to how the goal may be reached have already been offered, but these have yet to be brought together and presented as a unified theory.

Second, it was necessary to account for both the similarities and differences that surfaced in detailing the contributions of evangelical apologists. These were analyzed in terms of pre-cognitive and cognitive theories of philosophical disagreement. W.T. Jones offers a powerful theory that explains philosophical disagreements at the pre-cognitive level and points the way to balanced perspectives. Cognitive disagreements ultimately result from differences concerning epistemic justification. In this area, it is also possible to arrive at a balanced perspective through the application of a moderate foundationalism. Michael Czapkay Sudduth applies this approach to epistemic justification in a way that not only satisfies the concerns of coherentists, but also suggests how the transition from analysis to synthesis is to be made in apologetics.

On the basis of this groundwork, it is now possible to summarize and analyze contemporary evangelical apologetics on a more abstract level. By moving the individual apologists into the background and bringing the larger issues to the foreground, the theoretical outlines of the whole field emerge and become clear. The advantage of this kind of synoptic vision is that it boils down the details of apologetics to a manageable set of issues,

The Apologetics of the Evangelical Renaissance 114

alternatives, and principles. By mapping apologetics in this way, those who have become lost in the details of this complex field may not only find themselves on the map but may also find other places worth visiting.

The following summary is meant to chart the relevant features of the evangelical defense in light of the apologetic systems and underlying methods described in the previous chapters. After summarizing each issue, the methodological underpinnings of each alternative will be clarified. Because of the previous explanation of worldview orientations and theories of epistemic justification, there is no reason to elaborate at length on the connection between apologetic systems and their underlying methods. These connections are likely to be clear already, so the summary will simply confirm the lines that may already have been drawn by the reader. Due to frequent references to the basic schools or categories of presuppositionalism, the following abbreviations will be used: CP, Categorical Presuppositionalism; AP, Analytical Presuppositionalism; MP, Metaphysical Presuppositionalism.

THE SYNOPSIS OF APOLOGETICS

Basic Categories	Categorical Presuppositionalism	Analytical Presuppositionalism	Metaphysical Presuppositionalism
Presuppositional Scope	Minimal	Moderate	Maximal

Presuppositional scope concerns the *extent* to which presuppositions govern an apologetic system. Many apologists believe that one should presuppose as little as possible in order to avoid begging the question with respect to Christian belief. Though Christian theism may not be assumed at the outset, one may assume undeniable first principles from which an argument for Christianity may be derived. Thus, CP's represent this minimalist perspective. The MP's are on the opposite end of the spectrum because they presuppose the entire Christian system as a necessary presupposition. The AP's reflect the moderate position because they assume both epistemological and metaphysical first principles. They do not, however, presuppose metaphysical first principles as necessary to predication; rather, they believe that a worldview must be assumed in order to test its adequacy over against other competing worldviews.

In terms of worldview configuration, CP tends toward the static/discreteness/mediation poles, and MP tends toward the dynamic/continuity/immediacy poles. In general, evangelical apologetics avoids the extremes. Extreme examples fall outside the boundaries of argumentative apologetics. An example of an extreme form of the static/discreteness/mediation configuration would be Existentialism; an example of an extreme form of the dynamic/continuity/immediacy configuration would be New Age Mysticism. While AP seems to be the balanced position among the three, it actually tends toward the dynamic/continuity/immediacy configuration. The anti-empirical orientation of apologists in this camp clearly places them to the right of center.[1] Generally, evangelical apologists tend to be foundationalists, although MP's and some AP's embrace a coherentist approach to epistemic justification.[2]

Basic Categories	Categorical Presuppositionalism	Analytical Presuppositionalism	Metaphysical Presuppositionalism
Presuppositional Function	Categorical	Hypothetical	Categorical

The manner in which presuppositions are *held* is also critical to understanding different apologetic systems. Presuppositions are either held categorically or hypothetically. While CP's and MP's hold presuppositions in the same way, what they emphasize differs. A categorical presupposition is one that is necessary to knowing. In other words, it may not be held tentatively or experimentally. Without categorical presuppositions, knowing cannot get off the ground, so they must be taken as self-evident in some sense. While AP's share with CP's the belief in some foundational first principles that are held categorically, they believe that worldview assumptions must be held hypothetically. Christian theism is assumed "for

---

[1] Discreteness orientation is a major problem for the AP. Empiricism seems to isolate facts from one another to the point that there is no basis to relate them. Thus, Carnell's problem of empirical flux forces him to a Christian rationalism that puts innate ideas in control of empirical facts. Since the facts contribute nothing to their ultimate unity according to the AP, the discreteness/continuity orientation cannot be balanced. In actuality, CP is much closer to a balanced configuration because both facts and reason contribute to the unity of the facts.

[2] MP's would not often admit this since they do not allow for "neutral" epistemological methods. To admit that their position reflects a coherentist theory of justification would be, for many of them, an admission of neutrality that contradicts the presupposition of Christian theism as a starting point.

the sake of argument" and is tested by one or more complementary tests. The AP's see no reason to build a case for general theism as preparation for the case for Christian theism, as many CP's do.[3] Since Christian theism is what ultimately matters, arguments for general theism are of little or no value in apologetics.

On this issue, the mediation/immediacy orientation is relevant. Evangelical apologetics takes the mediation of knowledge very seriously, especially since the revelation of God is mediated. While Christian mysticism is prevalent in history, it is not prevalent in apologetics. The MP's come closest to the immediacy pole among argumentative apologists because of their strong emphasis on the universal sense of deity. Everyone knows God, but this is not pure immediacy because the revelation of God is a necessary medium or vehicle for this seemingly immediate knowledge.[4]

Of course, CP's and AP's also take revelation seriously, but it is balanced by an equal emphasis on language, logic, and sense experience as complementary means for knowing God. And since these other media may be employed to support conflicting belief systems, one should not adopt a worldview as an unquestioned starting point. Even the sense of deity is subject to error and distortion because of sin and fallacious reasoning, which provides all the more reason not to take a worldview for granted from the outset. While CP's believe that a general worldview can be established from first principles alone, they agree with AP's that Christian theism must be verified by its systematic consistency.

Basic Categories	Categorical Presuppositionalism	Analytical Presuppositionalism	Metaphysical Presuppositionalism
Presuppositional Content	First Principles	Christian Theism	Christian Theism

---

[3] Classical apologists believe that the argument for theism is necessarily prior to the argument for Christian theism; the evidentialist, on the other hand, believes that the argument for Christian theism may begin at any point, even though it often logically begins with the proofs for the existence of God.

[4] The doctrine of innate ideas among Christian rationalists indicates an immediacy orientation, but even innate ideas do not replace the *activity* of divine revelation as a necessary requirement in knowing God. This is why a Christian epistemology cannot be reduced to pure immediacy.

The issue of presuppositional content is likely well understood by this point but some additional elaboration is needed. As previously indicated, CP's do believe in presupposing Christian theism hypothetically in order to test its adequacy. But they begin with an epistemology of first principles. What has not been as obvious is that MP's must also make use of first principles, but these must be validated by the Christian system. Undeniability and utility are not considered sufficient to support them. Greg Bahnsen explains Van Til's position on logic:

> Van Til pictured human knowing as "thinking God's thoughts after Him." He also maintained that God's thinking represents perfect coherence. Therefore, in order for men to know things, taught Van Til, they too must think coherently or with logical consistency. *"The law of contradiction, therefore, as we know it, is but the expression on a created level of the internal coherence of God's nature."* So in all of our thinking about Scripture and the world, believers are obligated to think logically, thinking God's thoughts after him. *"Christians should employ the law of contradiction, whether positively or negatively, as a means by which to systematize the facts of revelation, whether these facts are found in the universe at large or in Scripture."* Van Til goes on to indicate that in contrast to unbelieving thought, the Christian views logic as a reflection of God's own thinking, rather than as laws or principles that are *"higher"* than God or that exist *"in independence of God and man."*[5]

For MP's, logic cannot be a starting point because it requires God to insure its applicability and universality. An impersonal background is insufficient to account for logic, which makes using logic to support an atheistic worldview absurd. While this is certainly true and all evangelical apologists recognize that God is ultimately necessary to account for logic, does this mean that we cannot begin with the laws of logic and other first principles? Indeed, MP seems to allow for this:

> In the process of knowing anything, man begins with his own experience and questions—the "immediate" starting point. However, that which man knows metaphysically begins with God (who preinterprets, creates, and governs everything man could know), and God's mind is epistemologically the standard of truth—thus being the "ultimate"

---

[5] Bahnsen, *Van Til's Apologetic*, 235.

starting point.⁶

Even though all knowledge necessarily begins in experience and MP's recognize this, they nevertheless affirm that the *ultimate* starting point must be an explicit presupposition from the start. For the other schools, the ultimate starting point is *discovered* in the process of experience rather than *postulated*. This is what accounts for the main differences on this issue, not the use of first principles per se.

At bottom, the discreteness/continuity orientation affects this question. The holism of MP's reflects a continuity orientation that favors a unified interpretation of facts. Facts are not taken as a discrete and yet related series that ultimately yields a unified interpretation upon faithful reflection (CP); rather facts must be viewed in light of a total system. The system, however, is not a mere hypothesis (AP); it is absolutely necessary to make the facts intelligible (MP).

Basic Categories	Categorical Presuppositionalism	Analytical Presuppositionalism	Metaphysical Presuppositionalism
Presuppositional Modality	Experiential	Logical	Transcendental

Presuppositional modality refers to the manner in which presuppositions are *used* in apologetics. The word *modality* refers to the way something is done, to a method of procedure. Therefore, in this context it refers the way in which presuppositions are used in apologetic argument. For example, the procedure of CP is experiential because assumed first principles are used to support reason and sense experience. Since first principles are the tools by which the Christian defense proceeds, it is important to establish the foundational principles that guide experience to a theistic conclusion. The word *experience* can be misleading because it may be used to refer to non-rational experience. But in apologetics, the term encompasses both reason and sense experience because both are necessary to knowledge for the CP. While CP's also share the method of AP's, the experiential modality is dominant.⁷

---

⁶ Ibid., 100.

⁷ In mapping apologetic systems, it soon becomes clear that the different schools share most things in common; differences are mostly matters of emphasis. In fact, it is disagreements on a few individual questions that create different emphases. For example, AP's care about first principles,

A General Summary of Apologetics 119

The AP employs a logical procedure because presuppositions are used to test worldviews as hypothetical possibilities. Hypothesis testing is essentially a logical method of determining whether or not a worldview is systematically consistent. The difference between a logical procedure and a transcendental one is based on what may be taken for granted by both the Christian and non-Christian. Given some common notions about reason and sense experience, the logical method of AP seems to be the best way to proceed with the Christian defense. But what if common notions are rejected altogether? Then it becomes impossible to do hypothesis testing because the Christian and non-Christian can never come to an agreement about the facts in order to determine what worldview best accounts for them.

This is why MP requires a transcendental method. The facts and their logical consistency cannot be accounted for by worldview testing unless and until we have an adequate philosophy of fact and logic to begin with. For the MP, the applicability and universality of first principles is more important than their logical undeniability, for undeniable principles are worthless if they do not apply universally.[8] And they are universally applicable only if they are transcendentally necessary. Only Trinitarian theism provides a basis for this, which makes knowledge impossible without the Christian worldview. Therefore, Christianity is true because of the impossibility of the contrary.

Again, this transcendental procedure is really not altogether lacking in the other schools. If Christianity may be established on the basis of the

---

but they disagree with CP's about the value of establishing theism from them. Therefore, they place a *dominant* stress on worldview testing because their main goal is to establish Christian theism, not general theism. Likewise, CP's agree with AP's that establishing Christian theism is the ultimate goal, but the ultimate goal cannot be achieved without reaching the immediate goal of establishing first principles and theism from those principles. This is in line with a basic premise of this study: Apologetic positions are better understood as points on a continuum than as discrete and isolated views.

[8] Of course, the CP would argue that the universal applicability of first principles is evidenced by their undeniability. Providing a larger metaphysical framework is also important to the CP, but such a framework is not necessary as a starting point. The CP proceeds according to the conviction that first principles are epistemically necessary to *discovering* what is ontologically necessary to account for them.

impossibility of the contrary, then why can't first principles be established in the same way? Since first principles are also required by the impossibility of knowledge without them, then they are, in fact, undeniable. And what of establishing their universal applicability? Are not first principles used by the MP to reason that Christianity is required to account for reason? In essence, the MP must accept undeniable first principles in order to frame a transcendental argument in the first place. The argument is based on "the impossibility of the contrary," which is just an expression of the law of contradiction—a first principle!

Basic Categories	Categorical Presuppositionalism	Analytical Presuppositionalism	Metaphysical Presuppositionalism
Common Ground Point of Contact	Epistemological	Epistemological	Metaphysical

The issue of common ground with the non-Christian is an important key to apologetic disagreements. This issue is also referred to as the point of contact because it concerns the point at which the believer makes contact with the unbeliever for apologetic purposes. The MP will tend to distinguish the point of contact from common ground because of the general belief among other apologists that common ground implies common notions. Since the point of contact for the MP is the sense of deity and not a set of common notions, the term *common ground* is either not preferred by adherents of this school or it is redefined to connote a common world rather than a common worldview. The MP acknowledges a common world of facts (metaphysical common ground), but not a common worldview or common notions (epistemological common ground).

Crucial differences about common ground proceed from different approaches to the interpretation of reality: Must the world be understood as a totality in order to be understood at all, or may the world be understood in a more piecemeal fashion? Given the undeniability of first principles, CP's see no reason to insist on a unified interpretation of the world as a requirement for knowing anything at all. Also, the substantial agreement between believers and unbelievers on many matters of fact seems to be strong evidence in favor of their view.

On the other hand, MP's argue that this kind of agreement actually results from the non-Christian borrowing Christian presuppositions without acknowledging their source. In other words, even surface agreement about facts is impossible between believers and unbelievers apart from the common use of Christian assumptions. The AP offers a mediating approach in which both common ground and the need for a totality perspective are acknowledged. But unlike the MP, the AP does not ask the non-Christian to accept the Christian gestalt as categorically necessary from the start.

Differences on this issue result from differing positions on the discreteness/continuity dimension. Much has already been said about the implications of this orientation for the interpretation of facts. In terms of a balance, CP and AP take a moderate position, and MP gravitates toward the continuity extreme. For the MP, a surface agreement about facts is of no real value to the Christian defense because the non-Christian views his facts within the context of chance and/or impersonal laws. Therefore, the facts, whatever they may say, will never speak of Christ to the non-Christian. Indeed, they can only speak against Christ. The CP and AP, on the other hand, agree with the MP that chance and impersonal law ultimately cannot account for the facts. But the facts themselves reveal this if they are viewed in terms of undeniable first principles and a verified gestalt. In the end, Christianity provides the only possible context for the facts (MP) or the best context among all the options (CP/AP).

Basic Categories	Categorical Presuppositionalism	Analytical Presuppositionalism	Metaphysical Presuppositionalism
Method of Proof Rational Procedure	Induction Deduction	Retroduction Abduction	Transcendental Argument

The method used to prove or warrant Christian belief reflects the presuppositional modality of each school. By this time, it should be clear that each school uses the primary method of the others, but each also has a *dominant* method. Induction and deduction are the primary methods of argument and are generally familiar to most people with even a basic understanding of philosophy. Retroduction and transcendental argument, on the other hand, are not as well understood. Since the nature of a transcendental argument has already been explained, a few words on retroduction will be useful in rounding out the picture of the rational methods employed in apologetics.

Retroduction is another term for what is popularly referred to as systematic consistency. It is also referred to as abduction.[9] Specific theories

---

[9] See John W. Montgomery, "The Theologian's Craft," in John W. Montgomery, *The Suicide of Christian Theology* (Minneapolis: Bethany Fellowship, Inc., 1970), 267-313.

and worldviews are usually not the result of induction and deduction alone. There is also an element of imagination involved in the use of logic, which searches for a theory to explain the facts in a way that induction and deduction alone do not. Whereas induction shows that something is *actually* operative, retroduction suggests that something *may be*.[10] Induction yields only "detail statements" about reality, but retroduction yields "pattern statements." John Warwick Montgomery quotes N. R. Hanson to explain the difference between these two kinds of statements:

> If the detail statements are empirical, the pattern statements which give them sense are also empirical—though not in the same way. To deny a pattern statement is to attack the conceptual framework itself, and this denial cannot function in the same way.... Physical theories provide patterns within which data appear intelligible. They constitute a "conceptual Gestalt." A theory is not pieced together from observed phenomena; it is rather what makes it possible to observe phenomena as being of a certain sort, and as related to other phenomena. Theories put phenomena into systems. They are built up in "reverse"—retroductively. A theory is a cluster of conclusions in search of a premise. From the observed properties of phenomena the physicist reasons his way towards a keystone idea from which the properties are explicable as a matter of course.[11]

From this explanation, a discerning reader will notice an obvious similarity between retroduction and transcendental logic. Is not a transcendental argument essentially a conclusion in search of premises and an attempt to build up a worldview in reverse? In fact, the two rational procedures are formally quite similar. At what point, then, do they differ? Put simply, retroduction suggests that something *may be*; a transcendental argument dictates that something *must be*. Retroduction offers a pattern statement that is *hypothetical*; transcendental logic arrives at a pattern statement that is *necessary*. Many who struggle to understand the precise difference between AP's and MP's notice the similarity in their rational procedure and remain confused because they do not see the difference

---

[10] Ibid., 274.

[11] Ibid., 275.

between hypothetical and necessary pattern statements. But with this distinction in mind, the difference becomes clear.

Basic Categories	Categorical Presuppositionalism	Analytical Presuppositionalism	Metaphysical Presuppositionalism
Extent of Proof Degree of Certainty	Practical Certainty	Moral Certainty	Logical Certainty

Each rational procedure involves a corresponding notion of certainty. In speaking of the extent of proof, it is important to remember that the certainty in question is that expressed in Christian belief. One may have logical certainty concerning a great many detail statements (especially those of mathematics), but pattern statements are another matter. Since pattern statements must be judged on their internal coherence and correspondence to a world of facts, the complexity of pattern statements makes it difficult to arrive at logical certainty using any rational procedure. It is important to remember that most apologists do not put all their weight on the rational leg. Spiritual factors are also involved in Christian certainty, which means that one need not feel apologetically betrayed if the argument for the Christian gestalt does not rise to the level of logical certainty. For if Christian faith requires more than logical certainty, then even an argument of this quality cannot guarantee an unwavering faith.

In terms of modest claims, CP is likely the most reserved with respect to its claims. Since deduction provides logical certainty of formal truths only, the Christian pattern statement cannot be deductively verified since it involves a great many material truths. Many of its historic details must be evaluated inductively, and induction does not yield logical certainty.[12] While the existence of God can be established with certainty according to classical apologists, the Christian God cannot be found at the end of a syllogism. Given the abundance of evidence for the Christian faith, however, the believer's faith is warranted. Therefore, the Christian is justified in having certainty because the evidence for the Christian faith is as good as the evidence can be for anything. Complete certainty, however, requires the witness of the Holy Spirit and faith, which together bridge any gaps in the evidence.

---

[12] See Ronald H. Nash, "The Use and Abuse of History in Christian Apologetics," *Christian Scholar's Review* 1, no. 3 (1971): 217-226.

In general, AP's may be characterized as commending a *moral certainty* on the basis of their apologetic defense. The term itself implies a deontological element with respect to the evidence for the Christian faith. The case for Christianity allows for no *reasonable* doubt, and therefore one *should* believe the evidence. Since the argument for Christian theism does not rise to the level of logical certainty, one still could doubt. But given the overwhelming evidence in its favor and the coherence of that evidence, one should not do so. Many CP's also explain certainty this way, but AP's tend to focus more attention on the element of the moral obligation associated with evidence.[13]

According to MP's, the case for Christianity is absolutely certain. Because Christian theism is transcendentally *necessary*, no other worldview is possible.[14] Therefore, Christianity is logically certain because of the impossibility of the contrary. The charge of formalism that is often brought against this view of Christian certainty has already been mentioned. Equally important is the fact that the charge of formalism is based on a discreteness orientation that makes it possible to doubt the connection between the world and our worldview.

The reason that MP's are seldom impressed by this charge is that their continuity orientation leads them to see the real and the rational as harmoniously related.[15] A balanced position on the discreteness/continuity dimension will appreciate the correspondence between the mind and the

---

[13] This kind of emphasis is very helpful for the habitual doubter. Many doubters have a sound moral sense that may be used to quiet their doubts. When the doubter concludes that the evidence for Christian theism is of such quality and abundance that there is no good reason to doubt, the habit of doubt may be conquered by the moral prohibition against doubting worthy evidence.

[14] It is important to remember John Frame's reservations on this point of logical necessity. Even if the evidence makes Christianity absolutely certain, our apprehension of the evidence and the arguments we make from the evidence are not perfect. Therefore, Frame really advocates the idea of logical certainty *in principle only*. Practically speaking, probability is still a part of the Christian defense.

[15] The MP's stronger immediacy orientation also plays into this. Immediacy orientation leads to the feeling that the mind and the world are naturally in sync. In more extreme cases, it will never even occur to this type of person to question the connection between thought and reality.

outside world, but it will not take the connection for granted. The connection must be supported evidentially as well as transcendentally.[16] In other words, the connection must be both coherent and correspondent.

Basic Categories	Categorical Presuppositionalism	Analytical Presuppositionalism	Metaphysical Presuppositionalism
Apological Schools **Notable Apologists**	Evidentialism Buswell/Geisler	Verificationalism Carnell/Ramm	Presuppositionalism Van Til/Frame

Understanding contemporary evangelical apologetics does not require a detailed study of every notable apologist. For purposes of summary, analysis, and synthesis, it is better to distinguish the major schools and establish the benchmark positions. While individual apologists have their own appeal and make their own unique contributions, most fit somewhere within the basic categories described by Hackett and the representative positions chosen for this study. To arrive at the goal of an apologetic synthesis, the important question to ask is whether or not the chosen representatives serve well to define the parameters of the field and discuss all the relevant issues.

Though only six major apologists have been chosen to represent evangelical apologetics, a number of other prominent apologists and their contributions have been used to amplify the contributions of those chosen for study. But of all the apologists referred to throughout this study, not one falls outside the boundaries established so far. Some might be classified as borderline cases between schools, but all share the same concerns and issues in common.

---

[16] Most apologists who appreciate the power of the transcendental argument type also insist on more traditional evidential arguments to support faith. MP's claim to do the same, but their conception of evidences is generally considered to be unacceptably circular. The appeal to evidence does involve some epistemological presuppositions. But most apologists assume only first principles as necessary to evaluating evidence in light of a hypothetical worldview. When the worldview that is to be verified by the evidence becomes a necessary presupposition of any appeal to evidence, then evidence loses its character as evidence and becomes logical entailment. In order to function as witnesses, evidences and presuppositions must be like witnesses in a court room. Though they share some common assumptions, they are nevertheless relatively *independent* witnesses to the truth in question. Each witness presents a different *perspective* on the truth, and no single perspective completely dominates the others.

Basic Categories	Categorical Presuppositionalism	Analytical Presuppositionalism	Metaphysical Presuppositionalism
Philosophical Parameters	Empiricism Aristotle/Kant	Rationalism Augustine/Descartes	Idealism Plato/Hegel

The philosophical parameters of evangelical apologetics are important for understanding the general philosophical orientation of each school. The term *parameters* is especially significant because each pair of philosophers represents the boundaries of the school with which they are associated. In a similar way, each pair of apologists represents the boundaries of the school with which they are associated. The connection between the philosophers and apologists, however, is not perfectly parallel. For example, the verificationalism of Carnell and Ramm may not be reduced to the rationalism of Augustine or Descartes. What is indicated by the parallelism is that verificationalism draws much of its philosophical inspiration from the rationalistic school of philosophy, which is best represented by Augustine and Descartes.

The similarities between philosophic and apologetic schools are largely formal. It would be unfair to label MP's as simply Platonic or Hegelian, since they are openly critical of both philosophers at many points. But the idealistic philosophical mentality has had an obvious influence on the shape of MP, just as the empirical mentality has influenced CP. These similarities are best accounted for in terms of the worldview orientations observed by W. T. Jones. Both classical philosophers and contemporary apologists have worldview orientations, and these result in formally similar positions where similar precognitive visions are chosen.

Even seemingly different positions within a philosophical school represent a common thread running between them. For example, the idealism of Plato differs in significant ways from that of Hegel. Plato believed that the world of forms is *more* real than the world of sense experience. Hegel, on the other hand, did not employ Plato's scale-of-being metaphysics, and so reality is not described in terms of more or less being. But both philosophers agree that the real (or most real) is the rational. MP's formally express this emphasis in terms of an epistemology of transcendental coherence. For Van Til especially, the rational governs the facts completely in a manner unmistakably similar to Hegel's idealism:

> Christianity is, in the last analysis, not an absolute irrationalism but an absolute "rationalism." In fact we may contrast every non-Christian epistemology with the Chris-

tian epistemology by saying that the Christian epistemology believes in an ultimate rationalism while all other systems of epistemology believe in an ultimate irrationalism.[17]

Van Til is careful to qualify himself by saying that this does not mean that mankind has a comprehensive rational understanding of God and all things. Instead, this comprehensive knowledge is in God himself.[18] But in referring to Christianity as an ultimate rationalism, Van Til aligns himself with the idealistic tradition of Plato and Hegel, which gives preeminence to rationality as the governing principle of reality.

Evidentialism and classical apologetics are also formally similar to the empiricism represented by Aristotle and Kant.[19] The primary influence of these two philosophers on Christian apologists is to be found mainly in the idea that reason and sense experience make complementary contributions to knowledge. Neither Aristotle nor Kant advocates innate ideas, but both affirm that something *a priori* structures sense experience. Kant comes closer to the doctrine of innate ideas than Aristotle does with his preformation theory of the categories, but neither takes this major step.[20] Apologists in the CP category reflect the same concerns and limits, carefully affirming *a priori* elements of knowledge without accepting the notion of innate ideas.

Verificationalists, on the other hand, make the move to belief in innate ideas, aligning themselves with Augustine and Descartes. Some do not even hesitate to refer to themselves as "Christian Rationalists." Among these apologists, Augustine especially provides the inspiration for much of their epistemology. Empiricism is strongly criticized as unworkable because it cannot solve the Problem of the One and the Many, mired as it is in the flux of experience. Even though the empiricist *discovers a priori*

---

[17] Van Til, *Defense of the Faith*, 58.

[18] Ibid.

[19] See Norman L. Geisler, "A New Look at the Relevance of Thomism for Evangelical Apologetics," *Christian Scholar's Review* 4, no 3 (1975): 189-200. Aquinas represents the most important classical example of this approach to knowledge for Christian apologists.

[20] See R. Eugene Gillmore, "A Reappraisal of Liberal Apologetics," *Religion in Life* 32 (1963): 369-379. This article provides a concise and interesting survey of how Kant's theory impacted apologetics.

elements in experience, these must be considered innate givens or they cannot rise above a conventional status to universal applicability.

THE ANALYSIS OF APOLOGETICS

By reducing argumentative apologetics to its theoretical issues and alternatives, it is possible to get to the heart of the key problems. As the previous synopsis has shown, evangelical apologists differ mainly in emphasis due to differing non-cognitive orientations. Important differences on a few substantive issues cause different orientations and are caused by them.[21] Differences in emphasis do not necessarily cancel out an underlying unity. A major emphasis for one apologist may be a minor one for another, but both apologists must agree on something in order to emphasize it differently. In the practice of apologetics, differences of emphasis are often required for diverse audiences. Non-Christians, like apologists, also have different orientations, and the wise apologist will discern these in order to present the Christian defense according to the listener's point of view. In reality, differences of emphasis are important to the flexibility of the Christian defense and its universal appeal.

While differences of emphasis are not really destructive of apologetic unity, some true differences must be resolved in order to demonstrate a substantial unity among the schools of apologetics. Based on the synopsis above, three issues in particular must be brought to a resolution in order to achieve the goal of the study. Each issue concerns a relationship between two things: (1) The proper relationship between method and content; (2) The proper relationship between categorical and hypothetical presuppositions; (3) The proper relationship between proof or warrant and certainty. Suggestions on how to specify these relationships have appeared throughout the study, but the total context has now been provided to bring all these suggestions together.

---

[21] There is actually a reflexive relationship between non-cognitive orientations and cognitive differences. Where a person comes out in belief depends on whether cognitive issues or non-cognitive orientations are doing the leading. Some people develop a non-cognitive orientation mainly from their reflection on cognitive issues. Others will follow what seems to be the natural orientation of their personality to its cognitive conclusions. In all cases, one's natural orientation affects the way one thinks through significant issues and vice-versa. But the dominance of one factor over another is relative to the individual personality.

Method and Content

The proper relationship between method and content is determined by two principles: (1) The method we use is shaped by a content that must be presupposed; (2) What we conclude from the application of the method must not constitute the sole grounds for the method. These two principles are at the heart of all that is acceptable in each of the three schools of contemporary evangelical apologetics.

Principle one would not be disputed by any Christian apologist. All recognize that some first principles must be assumed, or knowledge is impossible. Nor is there disagreement that Christian theism must be presupposed in some sense in order to verify it. CP's advocate a defense of general theism only as a support for historical faith, which serves as a stepping stone to saving faith. Evidentialists differ with classical apologists on whether historical faith in God is a *necessary* stepping stone or not, but they agree on the value of historical faith in most if not all cases leading to Christian faith.

The rejection of historical faith by AP's is an apologetical mistake. Both Carnell and Ramm deny the value of historical faith because it does not necessarily lead to saving faith in Christ. They also believe that coming to faith in Christ is not a two-step process from historical faith in God to faith in the triune God.[22] Their first contention is based on the idea that if

---

[22] Millard Erickson also aligns himself with Carnell and Ramm on this point but for a slightly different reason: "This new apologetic will not claim to derive a theism from the data of natural theology. Rather, it rests its content upon the special revelation claimed by Christianity. The contention is that once the hypothesis has been derived from the revelation, its tangency to the whole of man's experience can be seen. Natural theology is like a person trying to discover the solution to a mathematical problem from the problem itself. The new apologetic is more like a man who has been given a claimed solution to a problem and whose task then is to determine whether it is the correct solution. The Christian message is the key to understanding the puzzle of life. The case is not for theism in general; it is more effective when it seeks to assay the adequacy of the distinctive Christian biblical theism." Millard J. Erickson, "The Potential of Apologetics. Part II," *Christianity Today* 14, no. 22 (1970): 14. Erickson's point overlooks the fact that mathematical problems are generally solved by starting with the problem itself, and puzzles are meant to be put together piece by piece. He is simply stating a preference for working *from* a solution rather than *to* it and has not shown why the one approach is necessarily better than the other.

historical faith does not always compel Christian faith, then it is of no value in apologetics. This is simply false. In normal experience, people often progress by steps from one belief to another, and good pedagogical theory is based on this fact (cf. Isa 28:10). Fostering belief in God may not always lead to faith in Christ, but it may and often does.

The second reason for rejecting historical faith is also false. Ramm stressed that conversion to Christianity is usually not a two-step process. If we view a conversion from the perspective of the apologetic encounter that leads to faith in Christ, then, as Ramm says, we are not likely to observe a two-step process in which someone believes in God first and then believes in Christ as God. But conversions should not be understood so narrowly. For many, conversion is the culmination of a long history of experiences and reflections that lead to a final decisive encounter with a Christian apologist-evangelist.[23] Prior to the apologetic encounter, the person may have come to theistic conclusions on the basis of personal cosmological, teleological, and moral reflections. So even though the apologist does not present the case for theism as preparation for the Christian argument, the convert's own theistic reflections and conclusions certainly play a part in the eventual decision to embrace Christianity.

In reality, a complete and systematic case for Christianity is not usually required for effective apologetics. Unbelievers usually have a few main roadblocks set up against faith in Christ, and belief in God is usually not one of them. Where it is, arguments for the existence of God are a useful resource in helping atheists take a first step toward Christianity. There are many for whom the rationality of belief in God is of greater immediate importance than the systematic consistency of the Christian faith. Also, most reflective non-Christians tend to take their rational steps one at a time, which suggests that historical faith may actually be a natural stepping stone to Christian faith for many people. Judging from the number of people who come to Christianity from a general theistic belief, it seems unreasonable to accept the verificationalist's opinions about it.

Like the status of historical faith, the status of first principles also bears on the issue of method and content. It was observed that MP's also employ first principles in reasoning, even though they affirm Christian theism as the basis of all their thinking. In their thinking, first principles piggy back on the presupposition of Christian theism, which makes them

---

[23] See Frederic R. Howe, "A Comparative Study of the Work of Apologetics and Evangelism," *Bibliotheca Sacra* 135, no. 540 (1978): 303-313.

ultimately undeniable for the MP. In actuality, however, the MP must accept the undeniability of first principles *initially*, or reasoning from his Christian presuppositions would be impossible.

It is possible to argue that Christian theism rides piggy back on inescapable first principles, even in the case of MP. In fact, there is a reflexive relationship between first principles and the presupposition of Christian theism in MP. Each relies on the other for a different purpose. First principles rely on Christian theism for an ultimate justification; Christian theism relies on first principles for a rational explanation. Because MP's stress a unified interpretation of reality, they do not even recognize that first principles are as much a presupposition of Christian theism as Christian theism is a presupposition of first principles. For them, all that counts is the ultimate perspective. To view first principles as standing on their own in any sense is to violate the principle of unified interpretation, which is to say that it violates their continuity orientation. A balanced orientation, however, will recognize a distinction between the assumption of first principles and the assumption of Christian theism and will attempt to enlist both as complementary witnesses to the truth of Christianity. This is the rationale behind principle two.

Clearly, method and content are related in each of the schools of evangelical apologetics. All agree that a method involving first principles is not sufficient to lead to Christian theism. Christian theism must also be presupposed in some sense in order to verify its claims. We have also seen that the manner in which CP and AP presuppose Christian theism is formally similar to the approach of MP. Retroduction and transcendental logic both attempt to account for facts through a reverse process in which a cluster of conclusions searches for required premises. Also, the outcome of both procedures is the affirmation that Christian theism is required, either epistemologically or ontologically, to account for the facts. At bottom, the difference between MP and the two other schools is in the notion of epistemological necessity. Given Frame's concessions with respect to probability, it is even possible to argue for roughly equivalent notions of certainty among the schools.

Categories and Hypotheses

The notion of epistemological necessity is really what sets MP's off from all others. At this stage, the goal is to criticize those concepts that constitute the true points of contention among evangelical apologists. The relationship between method and content is really not at stake because everyone agrees that Christian theism must be presupposed in some sense in order to be verified. The controversy between CP's and AP's on the point of historical faith is also not at stake because AP's cannot support their rejection of historical faith on sound principles. And first principles are not at stake because they are undeniable. On the issue of presuppositional function, it will be shown that hypothetical reasoning also cannot be rejected on the basis of sound principles. If it can be shown that hypothetical reasoning is inescapable—even for MP's—then the notion of epistemological necessity at the heart of MP must either be rejected or modified to accommodate hypothetical reasoning.

Since CP's and AP's agree on the necessity of hypothetical reasoning, the focus here is on the argument of MP's, which is that presupposing Christian theism hypothetically subjects the Christian worldview to the autonomous standards of the non-Christian. In biblical terms, it amounts to failure in apologetics because it does not set apart Christ as Lord over the apologetic process (cf. 1 Pet 3:15). Since the non-Christian is invited to test Christian claims and decide for himself, it is argued that the non-Christian rather than Christ is really set up as Lord over the apologetic process.

Most evangelical apologists are not impressed by this charge because they do not recommend that non-Christians test Christian claims by just any standards and presuppositions. Standards of judgment and presuppositions brought to the examination of Christian claims are also subject to examination. Apologists outside the MP camp do not recommend a free for all when it comes to evaluating truth claims. Much of their work, in fact, is devoted to clarifying the difference between sound and unsound methods of reasoning. Thus, the claim by Van Til especially that other apologists are compromising the Christian defense by using Arminian or Roman Catholic methods really only serves to insult these apologists and fuels their antagonism toward his approach.

Among those who responded to Van Til's diatribe against hypothetical reasoning, Gordon Lewis probably offered the best response.[24] The main point of Lewis's response is that Van Til himself does not escape offering Christian theism to the non-Christian as a hypothesis. He basically faults Van Til for a kind of philosophical hypocrisy in which he criticizes his

---

[24] Gordon R. Lewis, "Van Til and Carnell—Part I," in *Jerusalem and Athens*, 349-368.

opponents for liberties he allows himself.[25] Lewis brings this out by comparing Carnell and Van Til on this point. Carnell proposes the Christian God as a tentative hypothesis to be accepted upon passing the test of systematic consistency. Lewis then raises the question: Does Van Til really assume Christian theism in a vacuum—apart from any concern for consistency or evidence? In practice, Van Til placed himself on his opponent's position for the sake of argument and then asked his opponent to do the same with his Christian position. This procedure is meant to demonstrate to the non-Christian that facts and laws are such only on the basis of the Christian position. At this point Lewis asks, "Is that so different from Carnell's invitation to the unbeliever to consider the logical starting point a hypothesis that makes sense of life in terms of intelligent coherence?"[26]

The point here is well made: There is no significant difference between a presupposition and a hypothesis when both refer to an assumption made for the sake of argument.[27] What then accounts for the difference in terminology? Usually the word *presupposition* refers to how the apologist holds Christian theism; the word *hypothesis* refers to how the non-Christian holds it. In actuality, MP's often confuse the manner in which they hold Christian theism with the manner in which the non-Christian will hold it for the sake of argument. Carnell as much as Van Til held his Christian beliefs as presuppositions because *for him* they were verified. Therefore, the AP sanctifies Christ as Lord just as the MP does. Carnell recognized that the non-Christian will not hold the Christian position as a presupposition until he becomes a believer.

---

[25] In a personal conversation I had with Dr. Lewis, he referred to Van Til's tendency to criticize others for following the methods of Aristotle or Kant when he himself was obviously following the method of Hegel. According to Lewis, this more than anything accounted for the many critics of Van Til over the years.

[26] Lewis, "Van Til and Carnell," in *Jerusalem and Athens*, 351.

[27] Francis Schaeffer is an interesting example of an apologist who preferred the word *presupposition* but often used it with a hypothetical connotation. Schaeffer's usage is legitimate because the word itself does not imply the manner in which something is supposed. Something may be assumed categorically or hypothetically. Perhaps Schaeffer chose to use *presupposition* rather than *hypothesis* because he realized that a person usually does not hold all assumptions in the same manner, which makes the word *hypothesis* too specific and technical for popular apologetics.

In practice, Van Til also recognized this, but because Christian theism is not *ultimately* hypothetical, he disliked the word and believed it should not be used in the Christian defense.[28] And yet, asking non-Christians to accept Christian assumptions for the sake of argument is an indirect affirmation of the legitimacy of hypothetical reasoning—a point Frame clearly affirms.[29] In suspending disbelief for the sake of argument, the non-Christian is not accepting Christian theism as a categorical assumption, and Van Til knew this. The fact that Van Til believed that Christianity alone is plausible and was willing to tell the non-Christian so at the outset only serves to obscure the fact that he was implicitly commending hypothetical reasoning.

So does Van Til really assume Christian theism in a vacuum—apart from any concern for consistency or evidence? Since Van Til consistently denied charges of fideism and voluntarism with respect to Christian presuppositions, we can only conclude that he does not deny the right, even the necessity, of testing Christian claims. Just as the non-Christian must suspend unbelief in order to consider the case for Christianity, so the believer must suspend belief in a special sense in order to determine whether or not Christian presuppositions are really necessary.[30] Thus, the Christian who puts his faith to the test must also use hypothetical reason-

---

[28] It is very easy to develop prejudices against certain words because they do not embody one's personal perspective. In apologetics, however, some of our terminology reflects the perspective from which the non-Christian comes to Christian claims. Buswell, who was at the opposite end of the apologetic spectrum from Van Til, affirmed that Christian theism *becomes* the presupposition of all one's reasoning once it is verified and accepted by faith. It is both possible and necessary to view Christian assumptions in two different ways depending on where we stand with respect to faith in Christ.

[29] Frame, *Cornelius Van Til*, 293.

[30] The Christian suspends belief for the sake of argument. This does not mean that he stops believing, but it does mean that he entertains the theoretical possibility that his faith is not reflectively justified or perhaps unjustified. Is it even psychologically possible to prove one's faith any other way? When Paul commanded the Corinthians to examine themselves to see whether or not they were in the faith, the test assumed the possibility, even if only theoretically, that they were not Christians (2Co 13:5-6). Paul trusts that they will "discover" whether they pass or fail the test by this examination.

ing in order to determine whether or not his faith is ultimately justified. We may assume from Van Til's own statements that there was never a time he did not believe in God, but are we to believe that he understood from birth that the Christian worldview is transcendentally necessary?[31]

In fact, Van Til, like the non-Christian, had to *discover* that Christian presuppositions are necessary before he could affirm them as such. Until he had an adequate basis to do so, the very idea could be nothing more than a hypothesis. This is not to say that his personal faith was hypothetical; the sense of deity and Christian nurture are sufficient to support Christian certitude even without a formal apologetic. But the transcendental necessity of Christian presuppositions is not an innate idea. The complexity and sophistication of Van Til's argument is evidence that it had to be hypothetical until it was fully developed in his own mind.

The point of all this is to make the answer to Dr. Lewis's question obvious: Van Til's presupposition was assumed to be true on the basis of consistency and evidence, and his presupposition had to be hypothetical until the evidence was sufficiently compelling to embrace it as categorical. *In the end, hypothetical reasoning is inescapable, even for those reflecting upon an existing faith.* If even the Christian must use hypothetical reasoning to arrive at necessary presuppositions, then how much more the non-Christian? Dr. Lewis was right: Van Til affirmed in practice what he denied in theory, and what he denied is inescapable. According to his own illustration, Van Til had to sit on Carnell's lap in order to slap him in the face.[32]

The controversy over categorical and hypothetical presuppositions reflects a false dichotomy in apologetics. In reality, believers and unbelievers hold assumptions both ways at different times. First principles are *used* by believers and unbelievers alike, but the moment they are examined to determine whether or not they are necessary, they must be held hypothetically for the sake of the test. Once they are approved, they are then embraced as categorical, or necessary to predication. Christian beliefs are generally taken for granted by unreflective Christians. They are taken as categorical for all practical purposes, even though the unreflective do not

---

[31] See Cornelius Van Til, *Why I Believe in God* (Philadelphia: The Committee on Christian Education of the Orthodox Presbyterian Church, 1948).

[32] Lewis, "Van Til and Carnell," in *Jerusalem and Athens*, 353.

understand what this means philosophically. Their Christian beliefs form the basis upon which they reason about other things, which makes them functionally categorical. Upon reflection, these beliefs are viewed hypothetically and eventually end up being viewed again as rationally categorical once they are approved.

All evangelical apologists end up with first principles and the Christian pattern statement as categorical presuppositions. They arrive at this point through a process of discovery and hypothetical reasoning. Categorical presuppositions, in simplest terms, are those that form the basis for all reasoning. There is, nevertheless, one final difference that requires attention. Though all apologists arrive at categorical presuppositions, there are still differences concerning the necessity of these presuppositions. Are the categories of Christian thought practically necessary or logically necessary? Perhaps different presuppositions are necessary in different senses. Different senses, in turn, imply different degrees of Christian certainty. A general theory of apologetics must also resolve this problem if it is to prove cogent and useful.

Proof and Certainty

In what sense are Christian presuppositions necessary? In logic, a deductive conclusion necessarily follows from true premises in a valid argument. If necessity is understood from this narrow logical point of view, then it can only be used in apologetics to refer to those presuppositions that are deductively derived. Since the Christian pattern statement is not purely deductive, it would be incorrect to speak of Christian theism as logically necessary. Logical necessity may also result from a transcendental argument by a kind of reverse deduction. If Christian theism *alone* can account for the world, then it would be appropriate to speak of it as necessary in a strict logical sense. The catch, of course, is that our lack of omniscience makes the word *alone* in the sentence above problematic. When we are sure of Christian presuppositions, are we expressing logical certainty or psychological certitude? And if certitude is really what we have, are we warranted in speaking of our beliefs as necessary because they are certain in this sense?

It is possible to speak of necessity in more practical terms, and apologists often do so. Christian beliefs become foundational for thinking, and in this sense function as categories that guide the reasoning process. Buswell, it will be remembered, defined presuppositions as *conclusions* arrived at on the basis of good and sufficient reasons. Since the Christian's "complex presupposition" becomes the test by which metaphysical propositions are proved, it functions as a category of thought and is necessary in this sense. From a strictly logical point of view, this kind of presupposition is not *necessary*. Instead, it is necessary according to the standards of proof approved by the apologist.

Even first principles are not strictly necessary. They are necessary because they are undeniable, not because they are indubitable or deductively derived. They are necessary to predication, but their number and the manner of their derivation and justification is not universally agreed upon. Like belief in God, first principles are basic, but they are also supported by higher-level beliefs that provide a mediate justification for them. These reasons are good and sufficient, but they do not demonstrate a logical necessity in the strict sense. Instead, they point to the necessity of first principles in a transcendental sense: They are not logically necessary; rather, they are necessary to logic. Transcendental arguments for Christian theism as a whole are similar. They are more complex, however, and it is more difficult to demonstrate the transcendental necessity of a worldview than it is a first principle or principles.

Apologists must reject the concept of logical (deductive) necessity with respect to the Christian defense and embrace what T.V. Morris calls "apparent necessity." Specifically, this concept of necessity connotes "the strength of the argument's adequacy, psychologically received."[33] Logical necessity is simply an unworkable concept for many reasons, most notably because it does not fit the dynamics of Christian certainty described in the Bible. Since logical considerations alone are insufficient to ground saving faith, even a logically certain case for Christianity would not prevail over unbelief.

---

[33] Thomas V. Morris, *Francis Schaeffer's Apologetics: A Critique* (Grand Rapids: Baker Book House, 1976), 35. Morris uses this term to describe Schaeffer's view of necessity: "I have used the phrase 'apparent necessity' both to preserve and to qualify Schaeffer's vocabulary. Preserving it yields insight into his attitude toward the argument, qualifying it yields insight into the relation between that attitude and the logical status of the argument itself. The conclusion of theism which has been reached is not 'necessary' in any deductively logical sense. At most it is highly probable as compared with atheism or naturalism. Thus the word 'necessity,' in distinction from what often seems to be Schaeffer's intention, cannot be used here in its logical denotation but only as it connotes the strength of the argument's adequacy, psychologically received (hence the qualifier 'apparent')."

As previously noted, a logically certain case also carries with it the liability of formalism. One can always doubt the connection between a rational construct and the real world. In fact, the more strictly formal a worldview is, the easier it is to doubt it. In the end, an apologetic of many witnesses and perspectives will always be stronger than an apologetic based on coherence alone. Whether that coherence is deductive (Clark) or transcendental (Van Til), coherence is only one perspective on the world and it is one-sidedly intellectual and formal.

In the end, a practical certainty that includes the deontological element of moral certainty is all that is required for a biblical apologetic and all that may be accurately claimed for any system.[34] Even John Frame realizes that Van Til's argument is not sufficiently transcendental to support the entire Christian worldview and its theology. Arguments of a more traditional kind are required, which means that Frame's approach, which is eminently useful and cogent, is not logically airtight by his own admission. If arguments yielding plausible results are part of the Christian defense at any point, then the standard of logical certainty is compromised. Ultimately, Frame's concessions are an admission that even MP cannot support claims of the logical necessity of the Christian worldview. Among those seeking to be biblical in their approach, this is not a problem.[35] Since the Bible's dominant apologetic model is legal, the biblical apologists were clearly not oriented to a standard of logical certainty.[36-37] Legal certainty is a form of practical certainty that commends proof beyond a reasonable doubt.[38]

---

[34] This practical certainty reflects the "apparent necessity" of the Christian system based on the perception of its existential undeniability.

[35] See Everett Ferguson, "Apologetics in the New Testament," *Restoration Quarterly* 6 (1962): 189-196.

[36] See Norman L. Geisler, "Johannine Apologetics," *Bibliotheca Sacra* 136 (Oct.-Dec. 1979): 333-343.

[37] See Merrill C. Tenney, "Topics from the Gospel of John Part III: The Meaning of "Witness" in John," *Bibliotheca Sacra* 132 (Jul. 1975): 229-241.

[38] See John W. Montgomery, "Neglected Apologetic Styles: The Juridical and the Literary," in *Evangelical Apologetics*, eds. Michael Bauman, David W. Hall, Michael C. Newman (Camp Hill, PA: Christian Publications, Inc., 1996), 119-133.

Among the apologists surveyed, Bernard Ramm presents a balanced and persuasive approach to Christian certainty. His distinction between spiritual certainty and factual probability fits well with the "apparent necessity" of Christian theism. An important observation stressed by MP's is that Christians do not hold their faith as a probability. This is absolutely correct, and Ramm's understanding of certainty affirms the point. For all practical purposes, the Christian faith is certain, even though the factual case is highly probable.[39] Some MP's view such an approach to Christian certainty as schizophrenic, and yet such a distinction is inescapable. Formalism and the burden of providing a comprehensive transcendental argument for Christianity leaves the door open to doubt and destroys the ideal of logical certainty in some versions of MP.[40]

Experiential Presuppositionalism

It should now be clear that a synthesis of contemporary evangelical apologetics is possible only if we criticize and reject a few major mistakes. A cogent theory of apologetics should not attempt to encompass what is indefensible and should not deny what is inescapable. As we have seen, logical certainty and the bias against historical faith are indefensible, and the use of first principles and hypothetical reasoning is inescapable in apologetics. On the basis of these resolutions, the positive contributions of

---

[39] See Jerry H. Gill, "The Possibility of Apologetics," *Scottish Journal of Theology* 16 (1963): 136-150.

[40] Hegel has often been faulted for failing to recognize that only an omniscient God could fulfill the project of Absolute Idealism. In a similar way, the MP is open to the same criticism. Even with the revelation of God, the finite apologist lacks the omniscience to know that his reconstruction of reality alone is absolutely and exclusively necessary. It may be the only adequate vision among the current options, but unless every detail of the worldview can be demonstrated to be transcendentally necessary, other variations would be possible. For example, a transcendental argument can be made for the Trinity. But without biblical revelation, it would not be possible to know from the argument alone exactly how many persons make up the Godhead. In essence, only the basic outlines of the Christian worldview can be supported transcendentally. Many of the specifics require special revelation, which, in turn, requires its own evidence for support. This is what Frame means in saying that Van Til was not sufficiently transcendental.

each school of evangelical apologetics may be affirmed as part of a unified theory of apologetics.

Given an adequate summary of apologetics and its qualifications, it is possible to select a term that best serves to describe a comprehensive presuppositional theory. Ronald Nash uses the term *Inductive Presuppositionalism* to describe an approach that embraces virtually all that has been concluded through this study. I believe, however, that the term *Experiential Presuppositionalism* is preferable and captures what Nash means by his terminology. When a scientist, literary scholar, or historian encounters a situation, text, or event, each must ask which explanation or hypothesis makes the most sense of the situation, text, or event. The evaluation of worldviews works in a similar way: "Honest inquirers say to themselves, *Here is what I know about the inner and outer worlds. Now which touchstone proposition, which world view, does the best job of making sense out of all this?*"[41]

While this description may seem to affirm no more than the familiar retroductive method of CP and AP, it may also affirm the transcendental method of MP understood in terms of *apparent necessity*. It was noted that the retroductive method of AP seeks the explanation that does "the best job" of making sense of our knowledge of the world. But does this imply any concept of necessity? If not, there is really no way to move beyond retroduction to transcendental logic. In what sense does Christian theism do the best job? Does it do the best job because other alternatives are unable to do the job at all, or does it do the best job among other plausible alternatives? Unless Christian theism *appears* to be the only option that explains the world, we have not moved beyond retroduction to a transcendental method.

John Frame offers an argument for the apparent necessity of Christian theism in the fourth chapter of *Apologetics to The Glory of God*.[42] Francis Schaeffer pursues the same goal in *He is There and He is Not Silent*. These examples echo Van Til's point, noted earlier, that the true theistic proofs attempt to show that the ideas of existence, cause, and purpose are meaningless unless they presuppose the Christian God. Frame is careful to qualify his argument by saying,

---

[41] Ronald H. Nash, *Faith & Reason: Searching for a Rational Faith* (Grand Rapids: Zondervan Publishing House, 1988), 63.

[42] Frame, *Apologetics to the Glory of God*, 89-118.

> My argument is not absolutely certain. Many readers will find problems in it. Certainly it is far from being a complete argument; at many points it could be improved by providing additional logical steps and clarifying some concepts. Yet it should have some persuasive value—granting that persuasiveness is very difficult to measure in apologetics.[43]

No further discussion of the arguments of Frame or Schaeffer is necessary to show that the idea of a transcendental argument understood in terms of apparent necessity has precedence and scholarly support. Even though such arguments do not rise to the level of absolute certainty, they do claim that Christian theism apparently does the best job of explaining the world *and is the only worldview that does*. This conclusion is consistent with the psychological certainty that accompanies Christian faith.

Experiential Presuppositionalism is a useful term to describe a unified presuppositional theory as long as it is remembered that the emphasis of the term is on *discovering* what must be presupposed and how such presuppositions should be held. As a unified theory, it is properly inductive, deductive, retroductive, and transcendental. Induction does not have a favored status over the other tools of reason and experience, which is why I consider Experiential Presuppositionalism the better term. The considerations of balance, which are central to the theory, provide for an apologetic with maximal resources and multiple perspectives. In practice, the theory has the power to demonstrate that Christian theism is both systematically consistent and apparently necessary to account for the world. With such evidence, what good and sufficient reasons could be given to doubt the Christian faith?

---

[43] Ibid., 90. Frame goes on to say that the testimony of God's revelation is certain, even though his argument is not. This contention could be viewed by some as essentially equivalent to Plantinga's idea that one is justified in holding belief in God as basic even without additional evidence or a perfect argument to justify it. Others, like Bahnsen, would ask how Frame could know that the testimony of revelation is certain when the arguments that embody that testimony are not. Frame would simply reply that the Bible clearly says so and then ask Bahnsen why he would even raise this as a problem for one who affirms Christian theism as the highest norm for all reasoning.

CHAPTER 7

A GENERAL THEORY OF APOLOGETICS

Contemporary evangelical apologetics represents one of the truly significant movements in the history of Christian thought and scholarship.[1] Evangelical apologists have not only offered fresh restatements of the arguments of the past; they have also attempted to bring a new level of clarification to the issues of Christian apologetics. The tremendous resources they have passed to the current generation of apologists demand the kind of synthesis attempted in this study so that everything of value in this movement may be put to its most fruitful use. Through its embodiment in a general theory of apologetics, the evangelical defense becomes a robust perspectival method.

It is unfortunate that evangelical apologists were not more concerned to discover their underlying unity. Much of the skepticism among apologists today concerning the possibility of a synthesis of evangelical apologetics is due to the divisive nature of the discussions among many of the scholars cited in this study. Differences of emphasis have not always been separated from substantial differences, and there has been too little concern for unity in a field where it is most needed. It has taken Christian analytic philosophers like Plantinga, Alston, and Czapkay Sudduth to provide the inspiration and ideas from which an ecumenical effort in apologetics may begin. The work of Czapkay Sudduth especially shows that evidentialists and presuppositionalists are not really as far apart as it was once thought.

What Christian analytic philosophers have done for the analysis of cognitive issues, W.T. Jones has done for the analysis of pre-cognitive issues. As one of the great historians of philosophy of our time, Jones

---

[1] See I. M. Andreyev, "Philosophy, Theology and Apologetics: A Brief Historical Introduction," *Epiphany Journal* 11, no. 4 (1991): 6-12. This article provides a brief survey of the history of Christian apologetics from the Eastern and Western Fathers to modern times. As an overview, it offers a snapshot of the context in which evangelical apologetics developed.

should be taken seriously. Where apologists have tended to view the difference between empiricists and rationalists in terms of the Problem of the One and the Many, Jones shows that there is something more to this controversy than a basic philosophical disagreement. There are also psychological factors at work. Although the Problem of the One and the Many cannot be reduced to differences in personal orientation, there should be no doubt that worldview orientations have their effect on this problem. Fortunately, the affirmation of *a priori* truths of divine origin is all that is necessary to resolve the problem, and all evangelical apologists affirm them.[2] Whether such truths are revealed through experience or are truly innate is a technical philosophical question and is not the linchpin of apologetic unity.

A General Theory in Principle

The analysis of apologetics in terms of presuppositions is, at bottom, easy to summarize. If everything said about the presupposition of first principles and Christian theism was captured in a straightforward statement, what would that statement be? In other words, what underlying principle should guide our reflection about what may be legitimately presupposed? Michael Czapkay Sudduth has already given the answer to this question. His principle of Bi-Level Evidentialism provides the best summary of what has been the guiding axiom of the study:

> Given any person S, if S's belief that Pc (where Pc = any Christian belief) is either (a) immediately justified, (b) mediately justified, or (c) both [(a) and (b)], and if p is either (a) or (b) then the correlative epistemic belief that **Pc*** is justified *only if* **Pc*** is based on adequate reasons.

This principle states that as long as we can offer adequate reasons for the epistemic correlates of our Christian beliefs, we can *show* that they possess positive epistemic status.[3] This principle distinguishes between a

---

[2] William S. Sailer, "Reformed Apologetics Revisited," *Evangelical Journal* 2 (1984): 23-24.

[3] Apologetics is about *showing* that Christian beliefs have positive epistemic status. One may be justified in believing something without being able to *show* the positive epistemic status of such a belief. This is the case for every Christian who cannot articulate the reasons for personal faith. One may be in a good cognitive state without being *aware* of it.

Christian belief (Pc), the correlated epistemic belief that Pc is justified (Pc*), and the reasons supporting the epistemic belief. As it is stated, Czapkay Sudduth's principle focuses on only one epistemic correlate, namely, how a Christian belief is justified (immediately and/or mediately). But other higher-level doxastic correlates are also available. Taking the Trinity as an example of a Christian belief (Pc), we might offer the following higher-level reasons for the positive epistemic status of this belief: (1) Belief in the Trinity *is a rational belief*; (2) Belief in the Trinity *is justified immediately and/or mediately*; (3) Belief in the Trinity *is formed in a reliable manner*; (4) Belief in the Trinity *is based on adequate grounds*.[4] Once epistemic beliefs (reasons) are stated in this way, we may then go on to give other reasons to support them. What reasons can be given to support epistemic beliefs about the Trinity?

Most would not consider belief in the Trinity to be immediately justified and therefore properly basic, although a case can be made for it.[5] For the sake of explanation, we will allow correlate number two above to stand as it is and attempt to give adequate reasons for the epistemic belief that the Trinity is both immediately and mediately justified. Reasons will be offered for all four correlates above, but not according to their stated order. Since some reasons will support more than one correlate, the argument will attempt to give reasons that together support all four doxastic correlates. As an example, the reasons that follow do not make up an air-tight justification that is beyond criticism, improvement, or additions. The argument is meant to be sketchy for purposes of illustration.

Belief in the Trinity is justified for at least three reasons: (1) It is taught by the Bible; (2) It is supported by the application of the first principles of existential causality and analogy; (3) It provides a sufficient and apparently necessary answer to the Problem of the One and the Many.

---

[4] Czapkay Sudduth, "Bi-Level Evidentialism and Reformed Apologetics," 388.

[5] See Nathan R. Wood, *The Trinity in the Universe* (Grand Rapids: Kregel Publications, 1978). In this unusual book, the author argues that the biblical doctrine of the Trinity is evident in the structure of the universe. Finding several trinities in nature, Wood develops what might be considered a cosmological argument for the Trinity combined with the principle of analogy. Because some of these Trinitarian patterns are immediately evident in our experience, one might argue that belief in the triune God is properly basic.

The Trinity is supported by biblical authority, which is in turn supported by a host of reasons for the Bible's inspiration and reliability. The principle of existential causality leads us to seek an ultimate source of personal community sufficient to account for finite community in the human sphere. The principle of analogy justifies our understanding this source to be personal like us, and yet this being must have community within itself because there can only be one necessary being.[6] These first principles, in turn, are justified by their undeniability, which is an adequate reason for accepting them as immediately justified. By applying these first principles to the problem of unity and diversity, we find that the Trinity meets the demands of the problem and appears to be the only solution that does. Since the Trinity is apparently necessary to solve the Problem of the One and the Many, it is also necessary to predication, which supports the contention that it is also immediately justified. But even if this reason is not considered sufficient to support the Trinity as immediately justified, along with the others it does provide mediate justification for the belief. Taken together, all these reasons show that Trinitarian belief is rational, formed in a reliable manner, and based on adequate grounds.

Czapkay Sudduth's principle implies what has been stated as a principle elsewhere: What we conclude from what we presuppose may not be the sole ground of what we presuppose. In other words, we must be able to give *other* reasons for our presuppositions *in addition* to what we conclude from them. This is simply to say that Christian belief may not be the sole basis for a Christian belief, which is vicious circularity.[7] All evangelical apologists are careful to offer epistemic reasons for their presuppositions in addition to the reason that Christianity alone provides an apparently

---

[6] "Two things, then, are entailed in the principle that Necessary Being causes being: First, the effect must resemble the cause, since both are being. The cause of being cannot produce what it does not possess. Second, while the effect must resemble its cause in its being (i.e., its actuality), it must also be different from it in its potentiality. For the cause (a Necessary Being), by its very nature, has no potential not to be. But the effect (a contingent being) by its very nature has the potential not to be. Hence a contingent being must be different from its Cause. Since, the Cause of contingent beings must be both like and different from its effect, it is only similar." Geisler, "First Principles," in *Encyclopedia of Christian Apologetics*, 252-253.

[7] See Clark H. Pinnock, "Karl Barth and Christian Apologetics," *Themelios* 2, no. 3 (1977): 66-71.

adequate context for them. For example, epistemological first principles are undeniable and evidence their utility in science and everyday life as well as in religion. Likewise, the metaphysical first principles of Christian theism provide a coherent, correspondent, and practical worldview, whereas other non-theistic worldviews prove unaffirmable upon examination.

In reality, the principle of Bi-Level Evidentialism is not so much a profound discovery as it is an astute observation of how apologists actually operate. In the end, the contributions of each school of evangelical apologetics were affirmed because all reflect this principle at the heart of their apologetic endeavors. Even Van Til, who is often labeled as a fideist, based his notion of proof on a higher level principle of epistemic justification.[8] Without question, his criterion of transcendental adequacy provides a powerful reason to presuppose Christian theism. But his version of this criterion claimed too much and proved too circular. For all practical purposes, Van Til's presupposition and the epistemic justification for it were virtually the same; instead of offering *other* higher-level reasons for a lower-level belief, he offered a lower-level belief as a higher-level reason.[9] Frame and Schaeffer, on the other hand, were careful to avoid this problem by not reducing epistemic reasons to a restatement of Christian presuppositions.[10] Frame's presuppositionalism boils down to the modest and

---

[8] See Stephen R. Spencer, "Fideism and Presuppositionalism," *Grace Theological Journal* 8, no. 1 (1987): 89-99.

[9] He did this by arguing that the criteria by which Christian theism is evaluated *ultimately* presuppose it, or else the criteria are meaningless. Therefore, epistemological criteria do not stand on their own *in any sense*. This blurs the distinction between higher and lower level reasons, which is consistent with Van Til's continuity orientation. A balanced orientation allows for epistemic level distinctions and *relatively* independent criteria. Criteria stand on their own as encapsulated reasons (discreteness) *and* they also call for an ultimate explanation (continuity). Narrow circularity is always an indication of a continuity extreme erasing or obscuring discreteness and represents the triumph of Unitarianism in epistemology. Ironically, the orientational conflict in Van Til caused by the influence of idealism prevented a consistent outworking of Trinitarianism in his apologetic; the balance of being and knowing was upset.

[10] See Harold A. Netland, "Apologetics, Worldviews, and the Problem of Neutral Criteria," *Trinity Journal* 12NS (1991): 39-58. Netland argues that Frame has not escaped an unacceptable circularity in his understand-

reasonable affirmation that criteria and conclusions must be *compatible*. Would any evangelical apologist disagree with this?

The problem of circularity raised by Van Til has been, in many ways, a great blessing to apologetics. In fact, there is obviously a dependent relationship between how we think and what we think. The methods we use and the conclusions we reach are related, as Van Til said. Christians should not be surprised to discover that God ends up being necessary to guarantee our reasoning. But as Hackett clearly argued, one does not need to presuppose the Christian God from the outset in order to reason. The *fact* of God's existence, not the *knowledge* of it, makes rational structure possible. In making this point, Hackett insures a distinction between presuppositions and higher-level reasons for them. One may even presuppose Christian theism in order to verify it, but this must be justified by epistemic reasons that are *other than or in addition to* Christian theism as a basis for itself. Christianity may be its own best defense, but it should not be its only defense.[11] Any use of presuppositions within these parameters is legitimate, and the principle of Bi-Level Evidentialism serves as an excellent measuring stick for apologists to check themselves.

The end result of Evangelicalism's concern with presuppositions in apologetics is the common affirmation that the Christian God is necessary to account for knowledge. While Hackett understands this necessity in the ontological sense and Van Til in the epistemic sense, the truth is that both perspectives are involved in the reflective rationality of the Christian

---

ing of presuppositions. In Frame's defense, he does affirm that Christian presuppositions are *pre* in terms of eminence, not temporal priority. This is why reasons can be given for them. While such reasons are not "neutral criteria," they do remove the stigma of "narrow circularity" from Frame's version of presuppositionalism. Frame's notion of "broad circularity" is simply an affirmation that criteria must be compatible with the conclusions drawn from them: "The point is that when one is arguing for an ultimate criterion, whether Scripture, the Koran, human reason, sensation, or whatever, one must use criteria compatible with that conclusion. If that is circularity, then everybody is guilty of circularity." Frame, *Apologetics to the Glory of God,* 10. This point hardly seems objectionable.

[11] See Stephen C. Evans, "Kierkegaard's Attack on Apologetics," *Christian Scholar's Review* 10, no. 4 (1981): 322-332. Evans re-interprets Kierkegaard in a way that makes a similar point. Apologetics does not seek to ground faith in rationalism; rather, it defends and interprets a personal faith already established.

believer. Christian theism appears to be the only worldview compatible with the use of reliable faculties, rational principles, and true knowledge. What is necessary as a *fact* for both believer and unbeliever becomes the *conscious* presupposition of the reflective believer.[12] In the order of knowing, the ontological always precedes the epistemological.[13]

This important apologetic insight did not originate with either Hackett or Van Til. Interestingly, both of these apologists were indebted to the great 19th Century Scottish apologist, James Orr. In tracing the roots of Van Til's transcendental perspective, Robert Knudsen gives Orr the credit for first developing this approach in Christian apologetics:

> Orr's method allowed him to begin with a confession of the Christian faith and to insist that it was the full Christian faith, not some preliminary religion of nature, that he was defending. It is, Orr claimed, the Christian faith that offers the presuppositions (postulates) which present us with the possibility of understanding our experience. The Christian faith thus becomes for James Orr the transcendental ground of our experience, that which provides it with its foundation and legitimation. Orr maintained that without these presuppositions experience would degenerate into chaos. There would no longer be any way to establish the ground of the possibility of experience. The only foundation for the order and the uniformity of nature is not something derived from our experience itself but is the absolute system within the mind of God. To strip away this presupposition and to seek within experience itself for a foundation is to fall into chaos. Similarly, the presupposition for the interpretation of history is the person of Jesus Christ. If one does not presuppose him as the source of meaning, the interpretation of history proceeds by an inner necessity down the road to irrationalism.[14]

---

[12] This is another way of reaffirming Buswell's point that Christian theism is both a conclusion and a presupposition. For the unreflective believer, it is a presupposition before it is a conclusion; for the reflective believer it is both a presupposition and a conclusion.

[13] There must be a knower and something to know before knowledge is possible.

[14] Knudsen, "Progressive and Regressive Tendencies in Christian Apologetics," in *Jerusalem and Athens*, 280-281.

Not only was Van Til's transcendental perspective inspired by Orr, but Hackett's was too. In reformulating the ontological argument for the existence of God, Hackett notes the similarity between his own approach and Orr's. Like Van Til, Hackett also recognizes the need to give an account of rationality itself:

> The question arises therefore: how are we to explain this adaptation of thought to the world of experience and this universality of the categorical structure? Since the categories are, in our experience, connected with a rational self, we may infer that their presence in the world and in other finite selves is to be similarly explained by reference to a Reason from which both finite selves and their world of experience are derived. In brief, the categorical structure of rationality and existence is grounded in the being of an eternal Reason or God.[15]

Considering that Hackett and Van Til represent opposite ends of the apologetic spectrum, it is important to note their common concern for the foundations of rational experience. Despite their differences on the issue, it is clear that both incorporate a transcendental perspective. James Orr published this perspective just before the end of the 19th Century, so it is not surprising that 20th Century evangelical apologists hotly debated the issue.[16] Indeed, it would not be going too far to say that this issue has been the central theoretical problem of evangelical apologetics over the last one hundred years. As a mediator for this conflict, the principle of Bi-Level Evidentialism seems to do the best job. Any transcendental perspective that maintains a distinction between lower and higher level reasons for Christian theism is valid; any perspective that blurs or eliminates the distinction is invalid.

A General Theory in Practice

Czapkay Sudduth's apologetic principle is not only useful to measure accuracy; it is also a license for creativity in apologetics. At the very least, apologetics is giving *one* personal reason for the Christian hope (1Pe 3:15). At its best, apologetics is giving *all* the reasons for the Christian hope.

---

[15] Hackett, *The Resurrection of Theism*, 192.

[16] James Orr, *The Christian View of God and the World*, 3rd ed. (Edinburgh: Andrew Elliot, 1897).

Between one reason and all reasons is a world of apologetic potential. If even one personal reason may be an apologetic, then why not develop special apologetic approaches for special audiences? In the end, the apologetic armory is as diverse as the perspectives of the modern mind.[17] As long as reasons are given and not forsaken for non-rational experiences, many possibilities are open to the modern apologist.[18-19]

Just as systematic theology plays a supportive role in biblical preaching, so a general theory of apologetics supports the activity of defending the faith. There is a distinction, therefore, between what Mark Hanna calls *Pure apologetics and Applied apologetics*:

> *Pure apologetics* is concerned with the objective justification of the Christian faith, irrespective of human response. *Applied apologetics* is the utilization of justificative procedures and data in the actual presentation and defense of the gospel. In contrast to pure apologetics, applied apologetics is marked by a high degree of person-variability. Since the purpose of apologetics only terminates in a ministry to persons, it is radically defective if it fails to accommodate itself to the work of the Holy Spirit in convicting and converting human beings.[20]

In *principle*, apologetics is limited by a general theory; in *practice*, apologetics is limited by an individual personality. Therefore, wisdom is required to discern which apologetic resources are best applied to the person or audience in question. In an interesting way, the six major evangelical apologists chosen for this study are apologetic prototypes of the

---

[17] Fisher Humphreys, "An Apologetic Armoury," *The Evangelical Quarterly* 48 (Apr-Jun 1976): 90-95.

[18] See Richard L. Sturch, "Fantasy and Apologetics," *Vox Evangelica* 14 (1984): 65-84. This article discusses the fiction of C.S. Lewis, Charles Williams, George MacDonald, and J. R. R. Tolkien as an apologetic for the Christian faith. The strategy of these authors is to remythologize, to appeal to mystery, and to overcome prejudice through an appeal to reason.

[19] See Clark H. Pinnock, "Cultural Apologetics," *Bibliotheca Sacra* 127, no. 505 (1970): 58-63. Pinnock shows how to use the dilemmas of modern man as a starting point for apologetics. The strategy of cultural apologetics is to show that these problems are best solved by faith in Christ.

[20] Mark M. Hanna, *Crucial Questions in Apologetics* (Grand Rapids: Baker Book House, 1981), 60-61.

non-Christian. Each has a mindset and orientation that determines what questions are important to him and what kind of answers are acceptable. There is a sense, therefore, in which each system of apologetics represented in Evangelicalism also appeals to a particular type of non-Christian. Unbelievers run the gamut from the empirically minded to the idealistically minded, and the wise apologist knows how to speak to them all.

Good apologists are like good chess players: They know the rules and strategies of the game, and they know how to apply them in contests with non-Christians. No two chess games are alike because no two opponents are exactly alike, which is what makes the endeavor interesting and challenging. Of course, apologetics is also unlike chess in important ways. The apologist does not play only to vanquish his opponent. Even though Paul uses military terminology when referring to our approach to non-Christian ideas, we should never engage in apologetic activity merely for the purpose of displaying intellectual prowess.[21]

The best way to protect against wrong motives and attitudes in apologetics is to clarify its objectives. Millard Erickson summarizes the potential of Christian apologetics according to ten tasks that serve as a practical mandate for the application of a general theory of apologetics.[22-23] Given the breadth and flexibility of evangelical apologetics, there should be no question about whether or not the resources are sufficient to the task. In light of over a half century of reflection on "the reasoned advocacy of the Christian faith," a practical mandate for apologetics is really all that is necessary to focus the gains of this useful movement in Christian scholarship.[24]

"What is the task of apologetics in this day?"[25] First, apologetics must ask the question of the *truth* of Christianity. Those who put relevance before truth get the cart before the horse: "In the long run, nothing can be

---

[21] "We demolish arguments and every pretension that sets itself up against the knowledge of God, and we take captive every thought to make it obedient to Christ." (2Co 10:5)

[22] Millard J. Erickson, "The Potential of Apologetics. Part I," *Christianity Today* 14, no. 21 (1970): 934-936.

[23] Erickson, "The Potential of Apologetics. Part II," 981-983.

[24] Erickson, "The Potential of Apologetics. Part I," 934.

[25] Ibid.

relevant that is not true."²⁶ Second, apologetics must show the *signification* of the Christian faith. In other words, the apologist must overcome the communication gap between the church and the secular world, making the Christian message as easy to understand as possible and being careful to avoid unfamiliar jargon. Third, apologetics must show the *significance* of the Christian message. Unless we can speak in the language of our hearers, it is unlikely that we will connect with their concepts and questions. Fourth, apologetics must define the *essence* of Christianity. Erickson explains this task in terms of a series of questions: "Is Christianity essentially an experience? A way of living? A set of doctrines to be believed? A series of historical events? Or is it several or even all of these, and if so, in what proportions?"²⁷ Fifth, apologetics requires posing pre-theoretical questions. Theology and apologetics assume some theoretical basis, but what philosophical categories are appropriate?²⁸ The attempt in this study to develop a general theory of apologetics is really a partial embodiment of this task. The questions to be answered are numerous and complex:

> A whole host of questions here arise. Does the Christian revelation carry a philosophy of its own? If so, how does one come to apprehend it? On what criteria does one judge which "pre-understanding" he ought to adopt? How can he become objective enough to make such an evaluation and choice? These again are hard questions, but they must be asked if we are to avoid undue distortion of the Christian message.²⁹

Sixth, apologetics should sharpen our thinking and focus the issues more clearly. This has also been a major goal of this study. By classifying and comparing evangelical apologists according to their presuppositional commitments, it is possible to bring evangelical apologetics as a whole into focus. As Erickson points out, "real progress in the resolution of differences of opinion can come only when the issue is correctly and clearly identified."³⁰ While such clarification does not guarantee progress

---

²⁶ Ibid., 935.

²⁷ Ibid.

²⁸ Ibid., 936.

²⁹ Ibid.

³⁰ Ibid.

or full agreement, "at least progress is more probable." Hopefully, the general theory of apologetics offered here represents a progressive step in the right direction.

Seventh, "apologetics also has a vital role to play in the spiritual well-being of Christians."[31] Because the focus of apologetics is mostly on how to persuade non-Christians, the equally important role of apologetics within the Church is usually not stressed. A reflectively rational faith is vital for Christian maturity, and the Church needs apologists for itself as much as for the world. Eighth, apologetics must develop empathy for differing viewpoints. The goal is not to destroy other viewpoints but to understand them. Only after understanding what others are saying can the Christian witness effectively. Dogmatism is unattractive in a Christian and violates the biblical requirement of gentleness and respect toward those to whom we give a reason for faith (1PE 3:15). Empathy must also be combined with humility, since "there is a difference between having absolute truth and understanding it absolutely."[32]

Ninth, apologetics must distinguish between the subjective and objective elements in faith.[33] Considerable attention was given to this issue throughout the study in an attempt to provide a balanced perspective. Faith is not purely subjective or objective; it is both. This is why Christian commitment cannot be reduced to the methodology of natural science. Scientific and historical factors must be considered right along with spiritual factors. Tenth, apologetics helps to place theology within the context of other disciplines. This is simply a way of saying that "apologetics attempts to relate theology to general culture."[34] Non-theological disciplines have always added depth to Christian beliefs. Secular history and archeology, for example, have deepened our understanding of the Bible, and philosophy has clarified our understanding of theology. Erickson also gives some good advice on how to use the contributions of general culture: "Neither uncritical acceptance nor blind rejection of culture should be the pattern for the Christian."[35]

---

[31] Ibid.

[32] Erickson, "The Potential of Apologetics. Part II," 981.

[33] Ibid.

[34] Ibid., 982.

[35] Ibid.

These ten tasks for apologetics provide a practical context for the general theory underlying the evangelical defense of Christianity. As practical guidelines, they accurately reflect what most evangelical apologists set out to do, and few would argue with any one of these suggestions. Apologetic controversy has centered on *how* to carry out these responsibilities, not so much on what should be done. The theory of apologetics proposed here is really an attempt to justify what most apologists do when they defend the faith. Because it is broader and more comprehensive than what any one apologist has proposed, the theory can include the individual approaches as valid perspectives on how to fulfill the practical mandate of Christian apologetics. As limited approaches, however, they come up short in showing the universal appeal of the gospel and its relevance to all mindsets.

The search for a general theory of apologetics is really an exploration of the psychology of faith. It is more than psychology because it deals with absolute truth, but it is psychology nevertheless. The factors involved in coming to Christian faith and being able to rest in that faith are complex and dynamically related. As people progress through life, the dynamics usually change. This means that the apologist aims at a moving target. People often go through phases in life, becoming existentialists, empiricists, rationalists, idealists, or mystics depending on their experiences and desires. They often incorporate more than one mindset in an uneasy tension. The questions they ask and the reasons that appeal to them change on the basis of these dynamics. By knowing how apologetics works, the Christian may present and defend the gospel of Jesus Christ skillfully, aiming for the heart of those in need of a Savior.

APPENDIX

THOM NOTARO'S *VAN TIL & THE USE OF EVIDENCE*

Many of Van Til's critics concluded that the use of Christian evidences is incompatible with his system.[1] The principle of circular reasoning at the heart of his approach certainly seems, on the surface, to commit him to a purely philosophical apologetic. Presuppositionalists have often countered this by pointing out that Van Til often affirmed the legitimacy of Christian evidences as part of the apologetic task. In an effort to explain and defend Van Til's position, Thom Notaro published a small book based on his Th.M. thesis at Westminster Seminary.[2]

Van Til & the Use of Evidence is an accurate and well-written defense of the presuppositionalist position, but Notaro leaves the critic with the same dissatisfaction concerning evidences that Van Til does. The major issue is simple: If evidences can say no more than Christian presuppositions allow them to say, then they do not witness to the truth of Christianity on their own. Indeed, some presuppositionalists who attempt to remain true to Van Til sound as if they agree with the critics on this point. Notaro quotes Jim Halsey who states the problem clearly: "The Christian can point to nothing outside the Bible for verification of the Bible because the simple fact is that everything outside the Bible derives its meaning from the interpretation given it by the Bible."[3]

While Notaro attempts to explain Halsey's statement in light of the pro-evidence perspective of Van Til, there is no doubt that some kind of tension exists here.[4] If everything outside the Bible derives its meaning

---

[1] See Clark H. Pinnock, "The Philosophy of Christian Evidences," in *Jerusalem and Athens*, 420-426.

[2] Thom Notaro, *Van Til & the Use of Evidence* (Phillipsburg: Presbyterian and Reformed Publishing Company, 1980).

[3] Jim S. Halsey, *For a Time Such as This: An Introduction to the Reformed Apologetic of Cornelius Van Til* (Philadelphia: Presbyterian and Reformed Publishing Company, 1976), 39.

[4] Notaro, *Van Til & the Use of Evidence*, 18.

from the interpretation given it by the Bible, as Halsey says, then any appeal to evidences is completely circular. Notaro does not deny this; in fact, he heartily affirms it as the position of Van Til. And yet, the circularity of evidences is precisely the problem according to the critics. If Christian theism as a whole must be presupposed in order to give meaning to the facts, then the facts do not testify to the truth of Christianity as objective witnesses. Notaro goes on to argue that the facts provide an objective witness to the truth, despite this complete dependence on the Christian system for their meaning and interpretation.

Notaro's explanation of this, while true to Van Til, exposes a conflict between the philosophical implications of Van Til's unified theory of interpretation and his theological commitments. Van Til correctly reasons on the basis of his theology that if creation is true, then there must be objective knowledge. Therefore, the facts do speak, but they do not provide the criteria for their interpretation.[5] The tension referred to above is revealed at this point. Traditional apologists are left scratching their heads, wondering how facts both speak and yet do not speak because they lack interpretive criteria. In fact, this very contention is merely the melding of Van Til's biblical theology and idealist epistemology. According to a biblical view of creation, the facts certainly speak loudly of God (ROM 1:20). But according to Van Til's unified theory of interpretation, they really cannot speak without a comprehensive system that interprets them. Evidence must be "shaped by a Christian interpretation."[6]

Lest the critics draw the conclusion (which they do) that Van Til's epistemology is derailing his theology, Van Til affirms his biblical belief that "God's revelation is everywhere, and everywhere perspicuous."[7] The question, of course, is perspicuous to whom, the Christian, the non-Christian, or both? In line with Romans chapter one, Van Til would say that God's revelation is perspicuous to both Christians and non-Christians.[8] But how can it be perspicuous when the Christian system is

---

[5] Ibid., 49.

[6] Ibid., 52.

[7] Ibid., 55.

[8] See David L. Turner, "Cornelius Van Til and Romans 1:18-21: A Study in the Epistemology of Presuppositional Apologetics," *Grace Theological Journal* 2, no. 1 (1981): 45-58.

necessary to understand every fact, and the non-Christian does not know or accept the Christian system? If Van Til says that the non-Christian is using the "borrowed capital" of the Christian to understand the facts, then the facts are still not doing the talking. Are the facts speaking for themselves, as Romans one seems to say, or is a system of belief speaking for them? This is a central problem with Van Til's theory of evidences.

Notaro goes on to discuss the similarity between Van Til's circular argument and modern philosophers like Quine, Alston, and Kuhn. Like Van Til, these philosophers "speak of the intimate reciprocity between transcendent norms and immanent facts." All these thinkers illustrate Van Til's idea of a "circular interplay between Christian presuppositions and Christian evidences."[9] While all this may seem to give presuppositionalism the backing of some of the best known epistemologists of our time, it is questionable whether these so-called supporters would say that every fact signifies that it is controlled by God, or else it signifies *nothing*. It is the all-or-nothing cast of Van Til's circularity that rubs other apologists the wrong way. If the facts say *nothing* at all without the Christian system, then who needs the facts to speak in favor of the Christian system? Indeed, they can say nothing for the truth until the truth says everything for them. Van Til's view of evidences makes them less than pawns in the chess game of apologetics. In the end, most apologists would say, "Why bother making it appear that you have something more than a purely philosophical apologetic when, for all practical purposes (for all evidential purposes), that is all you have?"

Most apologists agree with Van Til that evidences alone don't tell the entire story. The system that best integrates the facts provides the larger metaphysical context for them. But the facts say something on their own, even if they don't say everything. But to say that the facts say everything about God or they say nothing is going too far. Most apologists would agree that the relationship between presuppositions and evidences is "a circle of interdependence."[10] But it seems ridiculous to refer to facts as "manifestations" of the Christian system when they manifest *nothing*

---

[9] Notaro, *Van Til & the Use of Evidence*, 77. To Notaro's credit, his chapter on Van Til and verifiability is probably the best and most interesting chapter in the book.

[10] Ibid., 91.

without it.[11] Only if the facts say something can they manifest the Christian system.

In the end, Notaro's defense of Van Til fails to overcome the tension between the idealistic epistemology and the evangelical theology of presuppositionalism. Apologists often embrace philosophical views that seem to cohere with the Bible but which, in fact, are in direct conflict with it. *The necessary precondition of general revelation is certainly not brute factuality; but it is something more than mute factuality.* Notaro and some presuppositionalists are defending what is, at best, an unresolved tension and, at worst, a contradiction. This is why Van Til's theory of evidences has been controversial. The critics are really not failing to appreciate the interplay between presuppositions and facts; rather, they reject the complete domination of facts by presuppositions, and rightly they should. Put simply, some common ground between Christians and non-Christians is need to make a presuppositional appeal to evidences work.

Van Til, the philosopher, could have made his point more effectively by remaining consistent with what Clark Pinnock calls his "idealist coherence theory."[12] If the facts truly require the Christian system to say anything at all, then no appeal to evidences is necessary. The transcendental adequacy of Christianity alone is both necessary and sufficient to provide a formal proof of the Christian faith. But Van Til, the theologian, could not ignore the doctrine of general revelation and the biblical teaching that the facts of creation convey a perspicuous testimony to the true God. Therefore, he had to include a theory of evidences in his system. Unfortunately, the apologist of transcendental sufficiency was not sufficiently transcendental when it came to Christian evidences.

---

[11] Ibid., 87.

[12] Pinnock, "The Philosophy of Christian Evidences," 421.

WORKS CITED

Adler, Mortimer. *Intellect: Mind Over Matter.* New York: Macmillan Publishing Company, 1990.

Alston, William P. "Two Types of Foundationalism." *The Journal of Philosophy* 73, no. 7 (April 8, 1976): 165-185.

Andreyev, I.M. "Philosophy, Theology and Apologetics: A Brief Historical Introduction." *Epiphany Journal* 11, no. 4 (1991): 6-12.

Bahnsen, Greg L. *Van Til's Apologetic: Readings and Analysis.* Phillipsburg: Presbyterian and Reformed Publishing Company, 1998.

Barker, Kenneth L. and John R. Kohlenberger III, ed. *NIV Bible Commentary.* 2 vols. Grand Rapids: Zondervan Publishing House, 1994.

Bauman, Michael, David W. Hall, Michael C. Newman, ed. *Evangelical Apologetics.* Camp Hill, PA: Christian Publications, Inc., 1996.

Bernstein, Richard J. *Beyond Objectivism and Relativism: Science, Hermeneutics, and Praxis.* Philadelphia: University of Pennsylvania Press, 1983.

Burson, Scott R. and Jerry L. Walls. *C.S. Lewis & Francis Schaeffer: Lessons for a New Century from the Most Influential Apologists of Our Time.* Downers Grove: InterVarsity Press, 1998.

Buswell, James Oliver, Jr. *A Christian View of Being and Knowing.* Grand Rapids: Zondervan Publishing House, 1960.

_____. *A Systematic Theology of the Christian Religion.* 2 vols. Grand Rapids: Zondervan Publishing House, 1962.

Carnell, Edward J. *An Introduction to Christian Apologetics.* Grand Rapids: Wm. B. Eerdmans Publishing Company, 1948.

Clark, Gordon H. *Religion, Reason and Revelation.* Jefferson, MD: The Trinity Foundation, 1986.

Clark, Kelly James. *Return to Reason: A Critique of Enlightenment Evidentialism and a Defense of Reason and Belief in God.* Grand Rapids: Wm. B. Eerdmans Publishing Co., 1990.

Works Cited

Clark, David K. *Dialogical Apologetics: A Person-Centered Approach to Christian Defense*. Grand Rapids: Baker Book House, 1993.

Corduan, Winfried. *Handmaid to Theology: An Essay in Philosophical Prolegomena*. Grand Rapids: Baker Book House, 1981.

_____. *Reasonable Faith: Basic Christian Apologetics*. Nashville: Broadman & Holman Publishers, 1993.

_____. Review of *Apologetics to the Glory of God*, by John M. Frame. In *Trinity Journal* 16NS (1995): 127-132.

Czapkay Sudduth, Michael L. "Calvin, Plantinga, and the Natural Knowledge of God: A Response to Beversluis." *Faith and Philosophy* 15, no. 1 (1998): 92-103.

_____. "Alstonian Foundationalism and Higher-Level Theistic Evidentialism." *International Journal for Philosophy of Religion* 37 (F 1995): 25-44.

_____. "Bi-Level Evidentialism and Reformed Apologetics." *Faith and Philosophy* 11, no. 3 (July 1994): 379-396.

_____. "Prospects for 'Mediate' Natural Theology in John Calvin." *Religious Studies* 31 (Mar 1995): 53-68.

Edgar, William. "Two Christian Warriors: Cornelius Van Til and Francis A. Schaeffer Compared." *Westminster Theological Journal* 57 (1995): 57-80.

Elwell, Walter A., ed. *Handbook of Evangelical Theologians*. Grand Rapids: Baker Book House, 1993.

Erickson, Millard J. "The Potential of Apologetics. Part I." *Christianity Today* 14, no. 21 (1970): 934-936.

Erickson, Millard J. "The Potential of Apologetics. Part II." *Christianity Today* 14, no. 22 (1970): 981-983.

Evans, Stephen C. "Kierkegaard's Attack on Apologetics." *Christian Scholar's Review* 10, no. 4 (1981): 322-332.

Ferguson, Everett. "Apologetics in the New Testament." *Restoration Quarterly* 6 (1962): 189-196.

Flew, Antony. *An Introduction to Western Philosophy: Ideas and Argument from Plato to Popper*. New York: Thames and Hudson, 1989.

Frame, John M. *The Doctrine of the Knowledge of God*. Phillipsburg: Presbyterian and Reformed Publishing Company, 1987.

_____. *Apologetics to the Glory of God*. Phillipsburg: Presbyterian and Reformed Publishing Company, 1994.

_____. *Cornelius Van Til: An Analysis of His Thought*. Phillipsburg: Presbyterian and Reformed Publishing Company, 1995.

Geehan, E. R., ed. *Jerusalem and Athens: Critical Discussions on the Theology and Apologetics of Cornelius Van Til*. Phillipsburg: Presbyterian and Reformed Publishing Company, 1971.

Geisler, Norman L. *Philosophy of Religion*. Grand Rapids: Zondervan Publishing House, 1974.

_____. "A New Look at the Relevance of Thomism for Evangelical Apologetics." *Christian Scholar's Review* 4, no. 3 (1975): 189-200.

_____. *Christian Apologetics*. Grand Rapids: Baker Book House, 1976.

_____. *Baker's Encyclopedia of Christian Apologetics*. Grand Rapids: Baker Book House, 1999.

_____. "Johannine Apologetics." *Bibliotheca Sacra* 136 (Oct.-Dec. 1979): 333-343.

Geisler, Norman L. and Paul D. Feinberg. *Introduction to Philosophy*. Grand Rapids: Baker Book House, 1980.

Geisler, Norman L. and Ron M. Brooks. *When Skeptics Ask*. Wheaton: Scripture Press Publications, Inc., 1990.

Gill, Jerry H. "The Possibility of Apologetics." *Scottish Journal of Theology* 16 (1963): 136-150.

Gillmore, R. Eugene. "A Reappraisal of Liberal Apologetics." *Religion in Life* 32 (1963): 369-379.

Hackett, Stuart C. *The Resurrection of Theism*. Chicago: Moody Press, 1957.

_____. *Oriental Philosophy: A Westerners Guide to Eastern Thought*. Madison: The University of Wisconsin Press, 1979.

_____. *The Reconstruction of the Christian Revelation Claim: A Philosophical and Critical Apologetic*. Grand Rapids: Baker Book House, 1984.

Halsey, Jim S. *For a Time Such as This: An Introduction to the Reformed Apologetic of Cornelius Van Til*. Philadelphia: Presbyterian and Reformed Publishing Company, 1976.

Hanna, Mark M. *Crucial Questions in Apologetics*. Grand Rapids: Baker Book House, 1981.

Henry, Carl F. H. *Remaking the Modern Mind*. Grand Rapids: Wm. B. Eerdmans Publishing Co., 1946.

Howe, Frederic R. "A Comparative Study of the Work of Apologetics and Evangelism." *Bibliotheca Sacra* 135, no. 540 (1978): 303-313.

Humphreys, Fisher. "An Apologetic Armoury." *Evangelical Quarterly* 48 (Apr-Jun 1976): 90-95.

Jones, W. T. "Philosophical Disagreements and World Views." *Proceedings and Addresses of the American Philosophical Association* 43 (1969-70): 24-42.

Knudsen, Robert D. "The Transcendental Perspective of Westminster's Apologetic." *Westminster Theological Journal* 48 (1986): 223-39.

Kuhn, Thomas S. *The Structure of Scientific Revolutions*. 2nd ed. Chicago: University of Chicago Press, 1970.

Lewis, Gordon R. *Testing Christianity's Truth Claims: Approaches to Christian Apologetics*. Chicago: Moody Press, 1976.

Mayers, Ronald B. *Both/And: A Balanced Apologetic*. Chicago: Moody Press, 1984.

McGrath, Alister E. *Intellectuals Don't Need God & Other Modern Myths: Building Bridges To Faith Through Apologetics*. Grand Rapids: Zondervan Publishing House, 1993.

Meadors, John Thomas. *The Foundationalist Debate and Contemporary Christian Apologetics*. Ph.D. diss, The Southern Baptist Theological Seminary, 1993.

Mitchell, Basil. *The Justification of Religious Belief*. New York: Oxford University Press, 1981.

Montgomery, John W., ed. *Myth, Allegory and Gospel: An Interpretation of J.R.R. Tolkien/C.S. Lewis/G.K. Chesterton/Charles Williams*: John W. Montgomery, 1974.

_____. *The Suicide of Christian Theology*. Newburgh: Trinity Press, 1998.

_____. *A History of Apologetics Through the Centuries*. Class Syllabus: Trinity College & Seminary, n.d.

Morris, Thomas V. *Francis Schaeffer's Apologetics: A Critique*. Grand Rapids: Baker Book House, 1976.

Nash, Ronald H. "The Use and Abuse of History in Christian Apologetics." *Christian Scholar's Review* 1, no. 3 (1971): 217-226.

_____. *Faith & Reason: Searching for a Rational Faith*. Grand Rapids: Zondervan Publishing House, 1988.

Netland, Harold A. "Apologetics, Worldviews, and the Problem of Neutral Criteria." *Trinity Journal* 12NS (1991): 39-58.

Notaro, Thom. *Van Til & the Use of Evidence*. Phillipsburg: Presbyterian and Reformed Publishing Company, 1980.

Orr, James. *The Christian View of God and the World*. 3rd ed. Edinburgh: Andrew Elliot, 1897.

Pinnock, Clark H. "Cultural Apologetics." *Bibliotheca Sacra* 127, no. 505 (1970): 58-63.

_____. "Karl Barth and Christian Apologetics." *Themelios* 2, no. 3 (1977): 66-71.

Quine, Willard V.O. *From a Logical Point of View*. 2nd ed. New York: Harper & Row Publishers, 1953.

Ramm, Bernard L. *Types of Apologetic Systems*. Wheaton: Van Kampen Press, 1953.

_____. *Protestant Christian Evidences: A Textbook of the Evidences of the Christian Faith for Conservative Protestants*. Chicago: Moody Press, 1953.

_____. *The Christian View of Science and Scripture*. Grand Rapids: Wm. B. Eerdmans Publishing Co., 1954.

_____. *Varieties of Christian Apologetics*. Grand Rapids: Baker Book House, 1962.

_____. *Protestant Biblical Interpretation*. Grand Rapids: Baker Book House, 1970.

_____. *The God Who Makes a Difference: A Christian Appeal to Reason*. Waco: Word, Incorporated, 1972.

_____. *After Fundamentalism: The Future of Evangelical Theology*. San Francisco: Harper and Row Publishers, 1983.

_____. *Offense to Reason: The Theology of Sin*. San Francisco: Harper and Row Publishers, 1985.

Reymond, Robert L. *The Justification of Knowledge*. Philadelphia: Presbyterian and Reformed Publishing Co., 1976.

Sailer, William S. "Reformed Apologetics Revisited." *Evangelical Journal* 2 (1984): 17-25.

Schaeffer, Francis A. *The Francis A. Schaeffer Trilogy*. Wheaton: Crossway Books, 1990.

_____. "A Review of a Review." *The Bible Today* (May 1948): 7-9.

Spencer, Stephen R. "Fideism and Presuppositionalism." *Grace Theological Journal* 8, no. 1 (1987): 89-99.

Sproul, R.C., John Gerstner and Arthur Lindsley. *Classical Apologetics: A Rational Defense of the Christian Faith and a Critique of Presuppositional Apologetics*. Grand Rapids: The Zondervan Publishing House, 1984.

Sturch, Richard L. "Fantasy and Apologetics." *Vox Evangelica* 14 (1984): 65-84.

Tenney, Merrill C. "Topics from the Gospel of John Part III: The Meaning of 'Witness' in John." *Bibliotheca Sacra* 132 (Jul. 1975): 229-241.

Topping, Richard R. "The Anti-Foundationalist Challenge to Evangelical Apologetics." *The Evangelical Quarterly* 63, no. 1 (1991): 45-60.

Turner, David L. "Cornelius Van Til and Romans 1:18-21: A Study in the Epistemology of Presuppositional Apologetics." *Grace Theological Journal* 2, no. 1 (1981): 45-58.

Van Til, Cornelius. *Why I Believe in God*. Philadelphia: The Committee on Christian Education of the Orthodox Presbyterian Church, 1948.

_____. *The Defense of the Faith*. Philadelphia: Presbyterian and Reformed Publishing Company, 1955.

_____. *Common Grace and Witness Bearing*. Phillipsburg: Presbyterian and Reformed Publishing Company, 1972.

⸻. *The Works of Cornelius Van Til.* Logos Research Systems, 1997. Accessed CD-ROM.

Voss, E. John. *The Apologetics of Francis A. Schaeffer.* Th.D. diss., Dallas Theological Seminary, 1984.

Wood, Nathan R. *The Trinity in the Universe.* Grand Rapids: Kregel Publishers, 1978.

www.ingramcontent.com/pod-product-compliance
Lightning Source LLC
Chambersburg PA
CBHW071505040426
42444CB00008B/1509